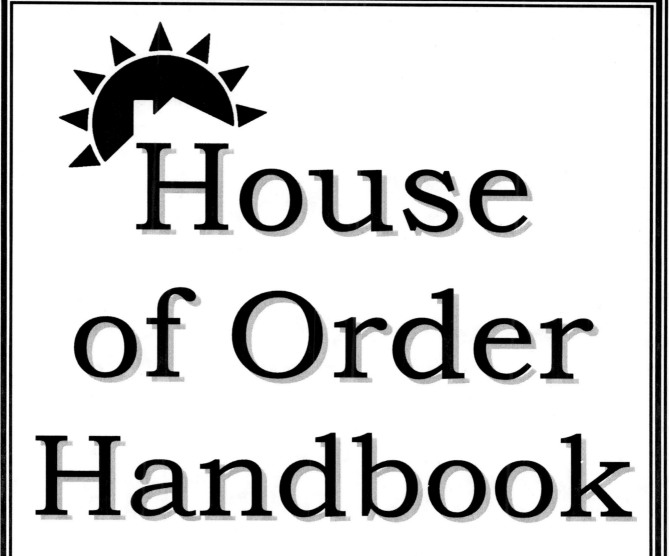

House of Order Handbook

Helping You Organize Your Life!

৪০৫৪

Marie Calder Ricks

2006

First edition.

Comments greatly appreciated: *www.houseoforder.com*

Also visit *www.houseoforder.com* for more
information concerning your organizational needs,
to purchase organizational products, schedule
a personal consultation, a speaking engagement,
or an educational seminar.

This book is dedicated to my loving husband and family:
Jim, Tom, David, Brian and Tyler Ricks

House of Order Handbook

TABLE OF CONTENTS

Chapter One

"HOUSE OF ORDER" PREPARATION

"Organizing is what you do before you do something, so that when you do it, it is not all mixed up."
Christopher Robin in A. A. Milne's <u>Winnie the Pooh</u>

SUPPLIES NEEDED:

Attached list entitled **Housecleaning Plan "Brain" Box Supplies, Worksheet #1**, is for a good start on getting organized. *page 4*

A more complete home organizational supply list is indicated on **Worksheet #2, "House of Order" Tools.** *page 5*

If you are ready to do it all at once, **Worksheets #75-82, Office Supplies List, Chapter #24**, include office supplies for all projects in this handbook. Other needed supplies are indicated in each chapter. *page 206*

GOALS:

Purchase or gather supplies needed as indicated on **Worksheet #1**

Label 3" x 5" card box as indicated on **Worksheet #1**

Label 3" x 5" card dividers as indicated on **Worksheet #1**

Time after time the story is always the same. There seems to be too much to do in too little time. There is too much stuff to fit in too little space. There is too much need with too little money. Why do we always seem to be on the short end of the stick? What can be done? Where should we start?

If you live somewhere and take care of someone, even yourself, you are a homemaker. I am a homemaker just like you. Almost everybody has comparable challenges, needs somewhat similar help, and benefits from the energetic application of certain principles and practices. So for over twenty years, I have worked with hundreds of women, teaching eight-week classes at local community centers, consulting in homes, lecturing at women's seminars, and presenting at Brigham Young University's Education Week in Provo, Utah and Rexburg, Idaho. This book and the techniques taught are a result of those many experiences which can now help you, too, become more organized. (You may also visit **www.houseoforder.com** *for motivational instructions, weekly tips, and proven methods to gain a more organized life.)*

In this book you will find stories and examples from other's lives. "Generic" names have been used to safeguard the privacy of those individuals with whom I have worked, but I share these stories so you will know you are not alone in the challenges you face. There will probably never be enough time, but we can understand how to deal with this limit. There will probably never be enough space, but there are ways to handle this challenge. There hardly ever will be enough money, but there are ways to survive and thrive past those limitations.

Are you ready? Let's go.

"House of Order" Preparation

Welcome to a new life, the life you have always wanted to live and have never known how, or maybe just never known where to begin, or maybe just needed someone else to tell you how to get going NOW.

This handbook is set up similar to a classroom setting. That is because, at times, you may find it best to tackle a project, especially something as big as household organization, a little bit at a time. You will notice each chapter is set up with **supplies** needed, **goals** to complete, and **instructions** on how to proceed including helpful **worksheets** to aid you. As you approach each new topic you will first gather or purchase your supplies, read through the goals and detailed instructions, and then go for it.

You may often find that facing your whole house at once is simply too overwhelming. So instead, in this handbook, you can face it in steps: simple, small, and easy-to-complete steps. You will notice as you skim through the handbook that you may start at any point and dig into a problem. Obviously it is easier to begin at the front and work through to the end, but if your needs are more in one area than another, it is all right to begin where you wish.

There are "preparation" projects which may be mentioned another place in the handbook which you may not have yet tackled. Their explanation and location in the handbook will be referenced for you should you choose to divert and complete a mentioned "preparation" project first.

So let's begin! Slowly, carefully, and without any fear, for it is time to make your life work better than it may have ever done before.

<u>First Things First</u>

First, you will want to purchase or gather several supplies to prepare the Housecleaning Plan "Brain" Box (see **Worksheet #1**). These tools are the beginning of gaining order in your home. After these supplies are gathered, your first goal is to prepare the "Brain" Box. Label the 3" x 5" card box and prepare the 3" x 5" card dividers.

The "Brain" Box is the location for all the housekeeping cards which you will prepare during **Chapter #15, Housecleaning Plan**, in preparation for keeping your home more orderly. You will add more cards to this box as you go along. (See **Chapter #12, Lists**, for more information.) For now, it is enough to have the box and label the dividers.

<u>The Second Step</u>

Second, after you have completed your House of Order "Brain" Box, there are several additional "House of Order" tools which make all the difference in your home, especially if they are used well. These are listed on **Worksheet #2, House of Order Tools**. Please purchase or gather these additional tools as your budget may allow. Each has a purpose which will be discussed later in the handbook. A complete list of needed office supplies for these additional projects is found in **Chapter #24, Office Supplies List**.

<u>The Third Step</u>

Third, as you become more confident and have the time and finances, even more "House of Order" tools can be set up. These are also discussed in later chapters in the book. Again, a complete list of all needed office supplies for all projects is found in **Chapter #24, Office Supplies List, Worksheets #75-82**.

Now to begin the transformation of your home! Remember, the first and most important thing to understand is that you are making your home orderly because you are interested in creating a haven of peace and security for those you love. The best place to start is to set up your own "home executive office", a place to plan and prepare for your new life. Good luck!

HOUSECLEANING PLAN "BRAIN" BOX SUPPLIES Worksheet #1

3" x 5" card box labeled "Brain Box"

3" x 5" cards, lined (at least 200)

3" x 5" card dividers labeled:

Daily	January	20_ _
Sunday	February	Birth Announcements
Monday	March	Birthdays/Anniversaries
Tuesday	April	Christmas Cards
Wednesday	May	Gifts Sent/Received
Thursday	June	Holidays/Special Events
Friday	July	Picnic Needs
Saturday	August	Trip Needs
	September	Visitors
	October	Wedding Announcements
	November	
	December	

"HOUSE OF ORDER" TOOLS Worksheet #2

Family "Information" Binder	Used for keeping current information in ONE place - for keeping essential information in ONE place - for keeping information about family members - for keeping household information - for keeping family medical information
"Finances" Binder	Used for master budget sheets - for monthly budget - for storing pay stubs, paid bills, and receipts
"Brain" Box (3" x 5" card box)	Used for tracking all daily and weekly household jobs - for tracking repetitive household chores - for tracking reoccurring yard chores - for tracking birth dates and significant holidays - for tracking picnic and trip needs
"Best Price" Box (3" x 5" card box)	Used for storing all "best" food prices - for storing all "best" non-food prices
Planner	Used for planning today - for planning this week, this month, this year - for planning menus - for tracking projects and writing down goals - for recording errands, thoughts, and "sources"
Large Wall Calendar	Used for tracking the family's routine schedules - for tracking the family's week-to-week plans - for tracking meetings, outings, and events - for tracking BIG family chores - for birthdays, holidays, and social commitments
Filing Box (large)	Used for filing important papers - for storing tax information - for storing instructions - for storing warranties
"Find a File" Box (3" x 5" card box)	Used for finding all filed documents

Chapter Two

THE HOME OFFICE

"Manage your home as a busy executive does the office. An office in your home or apartment is a TOP PRIORITY and you deserve it."
Donna Goldfein

SUPPLIES NEEDED: A large, flat surface

A small drawer or container for office supplies

A large drawer or container for filing papers
(This supply need is best met with a desk with several drawers [large and small] that can be used for handling written and thinking tasks, storing supplies and filing papers. However, circumstances may necessitate an adaptation. For instance, the kitchen table might be your desk, with a nearby kitchen drawer for your office supplies, and a cardboard box for filing your papers.)

GOALS: Clear out of the desk all expendable supplies and tools

Clean the desk inside and out

Purchase or collect necessary supplies and tools (see **Worksheet #3, Home Office Needs**)

Stock the small desk drawer(s) with supplies and tools

Stock the large filing drawer(s) with supplies and tools
need hanging file rack - bought one at DI?

Peggy was struggling. The few flat surfaces in her house, the kitchen table, the desk in her bedroom, and the top of her chest of drawers, were covered with everything imaginable: her husband's magazines, her children's school papers, her own lesson manuals, and many other pieces of paper which had long ago lost their identity and just become part of the many stacks. The sides of the frig and one of the kitchen walls were covered with post-it notes, some of which has lost their "stickiness" and had drifted to the floor. Peggy had no "paper sense". She was lost and she knew it.

It seemed an impossible task when I first came to her home. She couldn't find anything. She didn't even know where to start. She needed to handle paper work, but how?

"I know that if I put anything away," she explained, "I become very afraid I will forget to take care of it." That explained the wedding invitations, both current and some long past which covered the front of her frig door. That helped me understand the stacks of paper on the kitchen table.

How did she balance her checkbook? She laughed.

"I haven't balanced my checkbook in years," she sheepishly confessed. "My husband gets paid twice a month. I deposit his first check in one checking account and the second in another. I use up the first account's checkbook until I overdraw and then I use the second account's checkbook until the end of the month or when money runs out, whichever is first."

I almost giggled. I had seen some very interesting coping behaviors before, but I knew Peggy's ingenuity was going to make this a very interesting day.

I explained the reasons and purpose of setting up a home office. I helped her see that if she was going to be a professional homemaker, a great deal of her work would be at a desk. Everything we could do to organize her paperwork, set up a working area with tools and files, get rid of the papers stacked everywhere, those that wallpapered her frig door and the kitchen wall, would help make her home look a lot neater and also expedite the use of her valuable time.

She was willing, but not very confident. As a first step, we confined all the stacks of papers in produce boxes which we stacked along one wall of her bedroom. These she would go through as time allowed while her children were at school and the little ones were napping.

She decided to move the desk from her bedroom to a nook in the family room and set it up for her personal home office. I waited in the other room while she discussed this change with her husband on the phone. It was a short conversation.

"Anything you say, goes," she said, somewhat exasperated. "I guess my husband is so anxious to have things improve, he doesn't mind if we rearrange all the furniture in the house!"

So we moved the desk. We gathered tools for her new "office". She made a list of those she needed to buy. We found some file folders and I taught her concepts about confining mail and paperwork to folders so it was both convenient "to the eye" and yet "pretty".

We discussed when she would tackle regular maintenance paperwork every week.

"Mondays."

"O.K.," I said. "I'll be back Monday and we will walk through how it is done. For now, just put all the mail you receive in one place."

When I showed up on Monday morning, she was slow coming to the door.

"I just finished making the house presentable," she breathed heavily. "I think you will be pleased!"

Boy, was I ever! No only were the papers were gone, but the frig front only had the upcoming wedding announcements as decorations and there were no post-it notes out anywhere. Later I saw them in a large box in her bedroom, a project for later as she began to set up an address file. She had worked through two boxes of old papers during the last week and thrown most of them away. It was a great improvement and I knew we were well on our way to getting her set up as a professional homemaker with her own home office.

The Homemaker's Office

Do you need a home "office" to be an efficient homemaker? Yes! You are the executive of your home and you deserve an "office space" where you can think and work without facing a mound of clutter first. This is a top priority to getting organized!

A simple desk, well-organized and well-stocked, is all that is needed to have a home office. Properly prepared, it will save time and energy for it will provide a sense of order, in the beginning, to at least one small spot of your life.

What a Desk is Not

Your desk should not be a storage area for any items which will not aid you in your household tasks. Because we spend between 20-30% of our time looking for things, it will be important only those items that will aid your work should lie on the desk surface or be in the drawers. If you have to work around other "temporarily" stored items, it will not aid your work, for congestion prevents clear thinking.

Your desktop should not be a cluttered disarray. Remember, clutter breeds confusion. Your desk should not be kept clean by you just so it can accumulate someone else's daily clutter. All other family members can learn that your desk needs to be available to you upon demand. Their items of importance need their own resting spots.

Your desk area should not be a display case of distracting trophies, certificates, or intriguing pictures. The walls and shelves adjacent to your desk can, instead, hold tools and supplies to aid your concentration and reflection.

Need shelf/shelves above desk

What a Desk Is

Your desk should provide a place of quiet contemplation. It will be a place for decision-making, a "think" center. If possible, arrange to have the desk located in a room where the door can be shut occasionally for better concentration.

Your desk should be a place to handle paperwork. If it has several drawers, including a deeper, larger one for holding files, and a smooth surface for a phone and other tools, it can tremendously aid your organizational efforts.

Lastly, your desk should be a place to plan. A large wall calendar to record activities for all family members and a smaller, daily planner for your personal use will help keep the days rolling by with more effectiveness. A bulletin board to pin up business cards, dentist appointments and other notes will keep them safe until the information can be transferred to your planner and/or calendar.

The tools which will be most useful at your desk include those which are listed on **Worksheet #3, Home Office Tools**.

Practicing fingertip management as you store your supplies and tools in the desk area is important. Items within the reach of your extended arms when you are sitting at the desk should be those which you use most frequently. These might include the phone, calculator, and address file. Items which can be reached when you stand (such as binders, 3" x 5" card boxes and books on nearby bookshelves) should be those not needed as frequently.

The desk, itself, should be kept clear of all clutter except for the current task at hand. You will feel more in control because your mind, which can only handle one project at a time, will only be seeing one project at a time. It is helpful to have one drawer which is kept empty except to hold the current "project I am doing" which might easily be put away temporarily so you can handle other household necessities. This way, small hands or unknowing larger ones will not disturb papers.

There are several ways to handle the large, bulky phone books. My favorite is to tear the paper off a hanging file folder and insert the metal hanging bar into the middle of the phone book and hang it like a file in the large drawer. In addition, hanging your purse on the back of a nearby door keeps it handy for paperwork which must go in and out of it (checkbook, grocery lists, receipts, and cash).

Some homemakers simply do not have a desk and cannot get one in the near future. Their work area is often the kitchen table. In this case, using a kitchen drawer to store the basic supplies and tools will facilitate taking this drawer to the table when you "set up". A "filing" box might be stored conveniently in a nearby cupboard. If you can work near a phone and a wastebasket, paperwork will flow much quicker.

So, with a little effort, cleaning up, and stocking, you can set up your own "home executive" office, a place to begin being organized, really, really organized.

HOME OFFICE NEEDS Worksheet #3

Essential Tools

Uncluttered work surface

Small desk drawer (for supplies)

Large desk drawer (for files)

Light

Calculator

Wastebasket (large)

Rotating-type address file

Three-hole punch

Tool holder for:

    Pens
    Pencils
    Paper clips
    Letter opener
    Ruler
    Scotch tape
    Scissors
    Stapler
    Large eraser
    Glue

Telephone

Desirable Tools

Bulletin board

Large wall calendar

Pocket dictionary

Essential Supplies

Roll of stamps

Return address labels

Smaller stationery envelopes

Larger business envelopes

Stationery: Lined paper
                 Plain paper
                 "Scratch" paper

Postcards

File folders labeled: "To Do"
                        "Bills to Pay"
                        "Pending"
                        "To File"
                        Bank statements
                        Taxes
                        Vehicle Insurance
                        Home Insurance
                        Medical Insurance

Phone books

Banking papers: Account registers
                  Deposit slips
                  Withdrawal slips
                  Bank-by-mail envelopes
                  "New checks" box
                  "Used checks" box

Desirable Supplies

6" x 9" mailing envelopes

9" x 12" mailing envelopes

Post-it notes

Chapter Three

CLOTHES CLOSETS & OTHER CUPBOARDS

"Clutter creates confusion."

CLOTHES CLOSETS

SUPPLIES NEEDED: Bedroom clothes closet

Three large black garbage bags for:
- items to share with extended family or friends
- items which are useable to give to charity
- items which are "rags" to give to charity

Large wastebasket for "throw aways"

Large, empty cardboard box for items which belong elsewhere

GOALS: Empty the contents of the clothes closet onto a nearby bed

Organize contents into three piles: keeps, maybes, and discards

Return "keeps" to most accessible area of closet

Return "maybes" to less accessible area of closet and store under a sheet or towel

"Discard" everything else by giving or throwing it away

Put items which belong elsewhere in the large box

Susan was adept at so many things. She got projects done on time. She was hardly ever late, but when we visited she was frustrated and upset. Her closets and cupboards were all a mess, stuffed full of junk with no order or sense. She found out long ago that any house looks clean when it looks neat and easiest way to gain neatness is to put "it" away in a closet. The front room closet had all the right things in it: coats, boots, gloves, scarves, hats, and umbrellas but there were so many and it was so full. Not one item could be taken out without affecting the whole and causing an avalanche. Her own bedroom closet had some clothes hung where they belonged plus stacks of newly purchased items in bags on the floors, items stacked helter-skelter on the shelves above, and the look for a tornado. How was she to begin? There were no more empty closets in her home. At this point she felt she needed to keep every single item in every single closet. The new baby was coming in just two months and she was sure that would make it all much worse because she needed to get out the baby clothes but she couldn't remember whether they were stored out in the garage or in the attic.

She only had one month, in all practicality, to get her closets in control. How was she to begin and make any sort of progress without disrupting the already rather hectic schedule she was trying to keep up?

We talked. We came up with a plan. She promised to report back to me as soon as the first closet was conquered and then call again with each ensuing success. We got to be pretty good friends over the next few weeks for the energy she had applied in other areas of her life quickly transferred to this project once she knew how, when and what to do...

Clothes

Most of us have more clothing items than our closets and drawers will hold. This is because we tend to consistently add clothes to a closet that cannot grow accordingly. In addition, a large number of the clothes which have taken residence in our closets tend to be outdated, under-sized, or ill-fitting. Organizing your personal or any other clothes closet begins by setting a morning aside when there will be few interruptions, an unanswered phone and an easy-to-fix lunch.

First, find several, large black garbage bags, a large wastebasket and a large, empty box and bring them to the bedroom. Take all the clothes on hangers and pull them off the rod by armfuls and lay them in piles on your bed. Then remove the shoes and pile them together on the floor. Next remove all the other contents from the closet. Put these in a third pile.

Beginning with the first pile of clothes, sort through each item and ask yourself: "Is this a favorite piece of clothing?"

If yes, hang it back in the closet. A favorite piece of clothing is one which you wear at least once a week (in season). This might includes comfortable pairs of pants, favorite sweaters, or versatile suits.

If it is not a favorite piece, ask yourself: "Is it a maybe?"

If yes, hang it in the back corner of your closet. "Maybes" are clothes which you might want to wear again in the future but you can't right now because you are pregnant, want to lose a few pounds, or for which you need to find a matching piece. However, if you have not worn the clothes in the past year because they no longer fit, are a disagreeable color, or out of fashion, they are not maybes.

After you have gathered all the maybes into the corner of your closet, cover them with a large, old towel labeled "maybes". If you find you need one piece now and then, you can pull it out into the "keeps" portion of your closet. After one year's residency under the towel, it is time to give the idle "maybe" clothes away.

If the piece of clothing is not a favorite or a maybe, ask yourself: "Is it a discard?"

If yes, put the clothing in one of the large plastic bags. These are clothes which are useful but no longer needed. They are those which someone gave or bought you or you even bought yourself which do not match anything else, which do not fit, which are outdated, or which you have simply grown tired of wearing. Let someone else have some fun with them. Once they are gone, you will not miss them a bit.

Go through each pile of clothes on the bed, sorting by "keeps", "maybes", and "discards". Some clothes may be too old or worn to be useful, even to someone else. These go in the wastebasket or can be given to charity in bags designated as "rags".

You may also discover your closet holds items which belong elsewhere, such as a stray coat from your sister, or an item which might be better given to your daughter. These go in the large box. Do not leave the bedroom to put them away just yet because it is easy to get distracted from your main goal. Keeping at your task will get the project completed in a timely manner.

Out-of-season "favorites" should now be separated from the other "keeps" which are hanging in your closet. They are put together under another old towel labeled "out of season" at the other end of the closet. They could also be carefully stored in boxes in a storage room elsewhere in your home, if that is available. When they disappear under wraps, they also disappear from your mind. In a few months, when it is time to retrieve them again, it will almost be like having new clothes and will be more delightful to wear.

Shoes

After you have cleared the clothes from your bed, lay the shoes out in pairs on the floor. Ask yourself: "Which pairs are my favorites?"

Put these on the floor of your closet in two rows (if you are a shorter person) or on the shelf above your rod (if that is easier to reach). Those in the front are the ones you wear constantly. The ones in the back row on the floor are the ones you wear occasionally. If you have access to shoe boxes, put the shoes in open boxes. This keeps them together and keeps the area in a semblance of order. You can also purchase shoe organizers to help keep shoes easily accessible.

Those shoes which are leftover go in the give-away bag or the wastebasket depending on their usability. Remember, shoes get old, they get brittle, and they even seem to grow smaller (or maybe it is our feet that grow larger). If a shoe is not working for you now, it is no longer a tool, it is a guest. Let it sleep somewhere else.

<u>Everything Else</u>

After you have put away your shoes, go through the remaining items you have removed from your closet. Much of what we keep in our clothes closet should not be there at all, but are miscellanies which seem to have wandered in. Use your clothes closet mostly for your clothes and accessories. If there is extra room and you have non-clothing items which you desire to return to your closet, put them neatly away. But be sparing. It sure is nice to have more closet space than you need.

So now you have a cleaned closet. There are favorite pairs of shoes easily accessible on the floor or on the bottom shelf above the rod, favorite in-season clothes hanging accessible for your use, and two bunches of clothing under wraps, one "maybes" to be reviewed in one year, and one "out-of-season" favorites to be used in a bit.

Other useful clothing is in a bag to be given away. Garbage items are ready for discard, and misplaced clothing items are in the box where they can be transported to their new "homes".

<u>OTHER CLOSETS AND CUPBOARDS</u>

SUPPLIES NEEDED: A household closet or cupboard of any type

Two large black garbage bags for:
  - items which to give to charity
  - items to share with extended family or friends

Container for storing the "maybes"

Large wastebasket for "throw aways"

Large, empty cardboard box for items which belong
    elsewhere

GOALS: Empty closet or cupboard

Organize contents into three piles: keeps, maybes, and discards

Return "keeps" to the closet or cupboard if that is their best "home"

Store "maybes" in a sealed box in a less-accessible closet or storage area, date the box and label it as "maybes – discard in six months"

"Discard" or give away everything else

Put items which belong elsewhere in the house or need to be returned to someone else in the large box

Just as we work through and make decisions with our clothes closets, we need to be ruthless in ridding ourselves of useless trinkets and unneeded tools in our other closets and cupboards. The method is much the same, but it is important only one closet or cupboard be tackled at a time (to avoid too much disruption of the family's routine).

How is it done? A closet or cupboard is opened and all items are removed from it. This allows for a quick cleanup of the storage space. Then each item gets its turn for evaluation.

"Is this a favorite tool or trinket?" If so and the item should be kept, a second question needs to be asked.

"Is this the best place to store this item?" If so, back in the closet it goes. If it is a "favorite" but might be better stored elsewhere, put it in the large cardboard box for sorting later.

Next ask yourself: "Is it a maybe?"

This means you have some hesitancy about the value in keeping the item except that you may "need it later". Items of this type always provoke the hardest decisions. Maybe two further questions will help.

"Is it useful and will FOR SURE be needed LATER but is not needed NOW?"

If so, further thought must be given if it would be best to store the item for later use or to give it away and purchase a replacement (new or used) when the need does arise.

For example, clothes which might be useful for younger children might be better stored than given away. On the other hand, as your family matures, storing the crib for your future grandchildren's use must be considered carefully. What would be the better course: Give the crib to someone who will use it for the next several years and purchase another when those grandchildren arrive or have the crib taking up space in the garage?

Then comes the second question: "Is it useful but not needed in the foreseeable future?"

If so, give it away and let someone get the benefit of it. Most items which are useful but not needed now are best shared. Remember, anything that is kept is a burden of maintenance, storage and worry.

Those items about which you simply cannot make a firm decision should be stored in a sealed box labeled "maybes" and dated. The box is stored in the garage or storage area and given away <u>unopened</u> in six months from the time it was sealed. If you don't have reason to look in that box and retrieve an item in the next six months, you didn't need the items after all. Out they go.

Finally, ask: "Is the item a discard?"

If you haven't used the item as you had at first supposed when you either inherited or purchased it, and it has been taking its space in your closet without providing adequate benefit to your family, it is time for it to have another residence. Out it goes. Be frankly honest about each item. Most of what we keep we don't use, we just store. Let someone else have it and simplify your life.

After you have finished answering the questions about each item and put them in the appropriate container, you will have "keeps" in the closet, "maybes" in a labeled bag or box for temporary storage and possible later disposal, "discards" in the wastebasket or a large plastic bag ready to share, and items in the large box which go elsewhere. The items which are to be stored elsewhere are now put in the closet where they will most likely be stored (even if it crowds that closet for a bit until you clean it out, also).

So now you have the method for cleaning out your closets and cupboards. After you're done going through your closets and cupboards the first time, you will feel like you have moved into a new house. Occasional but regular cleaning out of your closets keeps the closets more useful, your junk level less disturbing, and your house definitely more in order.

Chapter Four

LAUNDRY

"Since it never ends, it might as well be as pleasant as possible."
Marie C. Ricks

SUPPLIES NEEDED: A laundry room or laundry area in garage

Wastebasket

Two-foot long towel rack (to "air dry" clean items)

Small pair or scissors (to trim threads)

Plastic tray (for stray socks)

Storage shelves

Plastic bucket (for wet items)

Shower tension rod or clothes hooks (for hanging clothes on hangers)

Two dirty clothes buckets for each bathroom: one for "darks", one for "lights"

A soft rug (for the floor where you stand to fold clothes)

GOALS: Supply laundry area with necessary tools to make doing the laundry easier

Decide upon the best techniques to expedite laundry completion

Figure out the best timing for doing the laundry to meet your family's needs

Melissa's life was a mess. It was mostly a mess because she couldn't figure out a way to get the laundry done in a timely manner. She had twelve children. The sheets hadn't been washed in so long one of her daughters commented they felt like a slippery slide. That did it. She called me to come help. When I arrived, I discovered a large appliance box which had been cut down to four feet high near the front door full of all kinds and colors of socks.

"If you need a sock at my house," she explained, "you climb in the box and get busy until you find two that match."

"Of course," she went on, "that rarely happens, but the children usually find something that is at least the same color and nearly the same size. They are lucky to get have clean underwear every other day and enough shirts to last through the week. Please, oh please, can you help?"

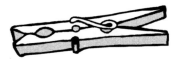

Tools

Doing the laundry is an "endless" chore which can be made easier with the use of the right tools, the right techniques and the right timing. First, prepare the laundry room by adding the right tools to make the job easy and convenient.

Place a plastic bucket near the washer for storing items which are wet, dirty and/or ready to be washed. This allows items which are used near the laundry room to have a "home" until the wash is done.

Next, provide yourself with a place to fold the clothes. This might be by putting the washer and dryer close together and folding the clothes right on top of them. (Sticking a rolled-up towel between the appliances keeps the socks from slipping down between the washer and dryer.) Or you might create a folding place by adding a table next to the dryer for sorting and folding. Just make sure that wherever you stand to fold laundry you don't have to bend over. Put blocks under the legs of the appliances or table to make them higher, if necessary. And wherever you stand to fold laundry, add a soft rug to ease your feet while you are folding clothes.

Install a 2' towel rack on the wall or under the laundry room's upper cabinets. There always seems to be a clean, but wet washcloth or a single sock which misses the dryer. This is also useful for holding empty hangers.

Put some sort of shelving over the washer and dryer to hold laundry supplies: soap, fabric softeners and stain removers, and the "strays" tray. If you buy powdered soap in bulk, you might want to store it such that the open bucket is next to the washer and at the same height. Usually, if you stack two closed buckets with an open one on top, you will get just the right effect.

If the laundry is located in the garage, put down strips of duct tape on the floor marking off the laundry area. Keep this area swept and make sure other members of the family keep this area clean of clutter. This will make the dirty laundry less liking to become smudged from garage dirt before it gets a chance to be cleaned and keep the clean clothes that way until they are returned to the house.

If possible, install some hooks in the walls or on the back of the laundry room's door. Or, alternately, hang a shower tension rod between two sturdy walls. As the clothes come from the dryer and are hung on hangers, they can be sorted with each family member's items hung in his or her own special place. Then when the family helps to put away their laundry (which is the best way to get it done), they can grab their clothes from "their" hook and put them away in their own closet.

A wastebasket should be placed close to the dryer for lint removal. A pair of scissors could be hung conveniently nearby for clipping threads which you might notice. A tray or box should be labeled "strays" for holding single socks for retrieval when the need becomes apparent.

Technique

The biggest trouble with doing the laundry routinely is that it cannot just be started, be done, and be over with. Instead, you must get it started in the washer. Then you wait. You must remember to transfer it to the dryer. Then you wait. Then you must pull it from the dryer, fold and sort it; and, finally, return it to its proper place. This many steps often befuddle the most determined homemaker.

It is best to start the laundry first thing in the morning if you are a stay-at-home homemaker. Purchase and set a timer for when the regular wash cycle should be completed (usually one half hour), transfer the laundry when the timer dings, reset the timer for when the regular dryer cycle should be completed if your dryer does not have a timer (usually 30-40 minutes), and then take the warm clothes from the dryer, separate them, fold them, and organize them for putting away. Another load can be put in the washer and the pattern repeated.

The working homemaker can use the same pattern when she does her laundry, whether in the morning or the evening, or she might split a load between morning and night. Sometimes it works great to get the wash started just as you go to bed and then dry it while you are fixing breakfast and getting off to work. Or, try putting in a batch in the morning and then drying it when you get home at night.

It is important to focus on "finishing" the laundry. So many women get started all right, but get stuck with wet clothes in the washer, dried and wrinkled ones in the dryer, or clothes heaped on the couch where they lay unfolded and frustrate the homemaker all day long. Finish the laundry completely while you are at it. When the timer dings saying the clothes are dry, remove them, sort them, fold them, and stack them for putting away. Family members should help with their own items, but having the laundry "done" for this final putting away is essential to feeling like you "got something finished today".

Gathering the dirty laundry is another matter all together. It is best to let members of the family help sort the laundry. Try putting two tall kitchen wastebaskets, one beige and another a darker color, in each bathroom. As dirty clothes are thrown down, they are put in the appropriate container according to their color. When it comes time to wash, the clothes can be dumped right in the washer (with a keen eye for an item or two that didn't make it into the right dirty clothes container). Using these same "wash buckets" for returning the laundry to its "home" with the aid of all family members, lets everyone participate. Laundry is one job which can be easily shared.

If you have small children or older "collectors", it will be wise to go through their pockets for "treasures" and trash. A wise mother teaches her children to do just that before they throw their clothes down with the advice that anything making it to the laundry room will have a new "owner", namely the laundry lady.

Socks can be a real hassle. The easiest method is to have each child wear only one color of socks during the week. The six-year-old wears white tube socks, the seven-year-old wears grey tube socks, and the eight-year-old white socks with various colored stripes. However, knowing girls especially like variety, it is also possible to have the seven-year-old with white socks with various stripes and the nine-year-old with solid pastel colors. If husbands are cooperative, having only one kind and color of sock for workdays really makes sorting socks less frustrating. Anything and everything you can do to make sorting the laundry easier makes for a faster laundry.

The same method might be applied to towels and washcloths. The dark blues are for the kitchen, the yellow for the main bath, and the beige ones for the half bath.

Children should be taught to help with the laundry as soon as they are interested in following their mother around while she does her chores. They can learn to sort clean socks, to fold washcloths, and to put items away. Giving each child in the family the opportunity to put away their own laundry plus one other set of items (like the kitchen towels and wash cloths) increases appreciation for mother's time in doing the laundry and alleviates many minutes during the week.

Timing

The laundry is best done routinely. This means deciding which days are for which dirty items. For instance:

On what days of the week will you do regular laundry?

HOUSE OF ORDER - LAUNDRY

On what day of the week will you wash the bathroom towels?

On what day of the week will you wash the sheets and pillow cases?

Most families work best if regular laundry (lights, mediums and darks) are washed Monday/Wednesday/Friday. If the schedule is such that no one is home during the day, the laundry might be started early in the morning by one person and then dried, folded and put away by others when family members return. Or alternately, the laundry could be started in the evening and then dried and hung in the early morning with different members of the family in charge of each part of the whole process.

Bath towels might be washed on Tuesday and bedding on Thursday. This leaves Saturday morning for miscellaneous items such as gym clothes, and large, infrequently washed items such as bedspreads, drapes, or rugs.

On laundry day, the person who begins it collects the dirty clothes buckets from the bathrooms, begins the laundry, and returns to other chores. When the items have been folded, they can be sorted back into the wash buckets, and family members can help return the clean items to where they belong. Each family member has his or her own wash bucket of clean clothes to put away before he returns the bucket to its bathroom "home".

This also avoids the problem of children who put slightly used but still clean clothes down to be washed instead of returning them to their closet (to save themselves some hassle). It is hard to get excited about giving yourself more work.

Even young children can begin helping with the laundry. When a child turns two, he or she is ready to regularly participate in putting his or her dirty clothes in the appropriate wash bucket and returning his or her clean undershirts, tops, and pants to his or her drawers. Such early training will do a great deal to help any child desire to be neat and clean as he or she matures.

Remember, the laundry need not be tedious, unfulfilling or dull. It is endless, but the load is lightened with a regular routine and shared duties.

Chapter Five

COPING WITH CLUTTER

"90% of life is maintenance, 90% of
housework is picking up."

SUPPLIES NEEDED: **"Coping with Clutter", Worksheet #4**

GOALS: Complete the "Coping with Clutter" worksheet to identify
areas of concern

Set up convenient places to "throw away" (i.e.,
wastebaskets), to "hold for review" (i.e., mail slot), to "put
away later" (i.e., shelf where each family member can find
items they have left around the house which have been
picked up for them)

Hold a family council to explain new procedures and elicit
cooperation of everyone living in the home (see **Chapter #11,
Family Councils**, for further details)

Teach consistent "coping with clutter" principles by
encouraging others' participation and offering incentives

Begin the habit of straightening up the house at least twice
each day

     *Sherri's house was nothing more than a series of tunnels. I didn't call it a
"mole's home". She did. When she showed up to class the first week, she
explained her husband was a collector, a real-time collector. He saved
everything, every time. He saved newspapers, magazines, and empty milk
cartons. (She was pleased to report he did wash them out before sticking them
on the back porch.) He saved rubber bands and boxes and margarine tubs.*
     *He apparently had been in charge of emptying the wastebaskets as a
child and had hated the job. She wondered if that had anything to do with his
abhorrence with throwing away now. It had gotten so bad that most of their
home was completely stuffed with things which were too valuable, either for
immediate use or most likely for future use, that they lived by walking down
"tunnels" in some of the rooms. The garage was completely full and they parked*

the car outside. The back yard had its share of stuff, too. It wasn't a big house, to be sure, she said, but did they really need to keep so much stuff?

When I visited with her at her home, we sat on the edge of her front porch. Even it was covered with too many things to name and she really didn't want me to come into the house quite yet. Her husband realized he could never throw anything away, and yet sensing that something had to be done, he had given her permission to seek help.

And so we talked. I explained. She understood. We set limits on "gathering". We decided how to begin... It was fun for me, liberating for her, and terrifying for her husband (although later he thanked me for giving him someone to blame for the loss of his many "special" treasures).

The Front Room

Where do you begin to make your own home orderly? The most beneficial is the area adjacent to the front door (usually the living room). This is because an unkempt living room is most embarrassing when unexpected company shows up and is the room first seen by visitors coming into the house.

Family members grow used to a certain level of clutter in the house. It is important to begin 'decluttering" in a room which offers immediate benefits. If none of the other rooms are free of clutter, having the living room presentable will relieve a great deal of stress in your life, offer a place of cleanliness and order, and give the family a sense of comfort because visitors are unaware of the realities beyond the front room.

To begin, list on the accompanying "Coping With Clutter" worksheet (**Worksheet #4**) the items which you currently find in your living room which seem to always be there. Is it your son's tennis shoes, this morning's paper, magazines your daughter has been reading? Then indicate in the second column which family members will be regularly responsible to see that these offending items are put back in their "home".

Before items will regularly be put away, they must have a place to call their home. Does your son have a specific place in his closet for his shoes? Does your husband have a convenient place to put the newspaper after he reads it in the morning? Does your daughter have a handy place for her latest magazines? If not, designate where each of these items belongs in the third column of the worksheet.

In addition, deciding how often family members are responsible for putting away their items is very helpful to maintain a "de-cluttered" room. It is suggested the living room be picked up before family members leave in the morning and again before everyone goes to bed. As this becomes a regular habit, the room will stay in reasonable order. Indicate in the fourth column when during the day the "cluttering" items will be returned to their "homes".

For one week, post the "Coping with Clutter" Worksheet on the refrigerator, and concentrate on keeping the living room picked up. In order to get habits established, each family member tries to put away their items morning and night without being asked. If one family member is at home regularly, he could be responsible to retrieve items which have not been picked up as requested. These items might be "bought" back by doing an extra chore, volunteering to help with the dishes, or picking up a certain number of other misplaced items.

One family had a "buy-back" box. For example, if you are fourteen and you leave your dirty shirt on the back of the couch and go to bed, then you must buy it back the next day by picking up fourteen other "misplaced" items, helping with the dinner dishes, or sweeping the front porch.

Another game to play with children (old and young) is helpful. Items which are left out become property of the "housekeeper" for one day. Then family members are able to retrieve their items from the "clutter" box and try again. If the item is left out a second time, then it is unavailable for two days. If the items are essential for school or work, then the item is retrievable if other misplaced items or toys are picked to "pay" for the necessary item.

If the living room is picked up last thing before school-age children and working members leave and then again before they go to bed, it has a decent chance to survive as an orderly room.

Bedrooms

After the living room has been kept orderly for a week, it is time to concentrate on the children's bedrooms. A certain time each week, usually on Saturdays, is set aside for straightening up, dusting, and controlling clutter.

Initially, it is best for an adult to help younger children with these jobs. This gives them a chance to learn proper principles about emptying wastebaskets, dusting shelves, distinguishing between school papers to save in a journal and those to throw out, sorting through treasures to keep and discarding the rest.

Helping children with their rooms also gives parents an intimate opportunity to teach simple principles of orderliness about hanging clothes in the closet, folding clothes in the chest of drawers, and straightening the desk area. Caring about the orderliness of a child's room even as you help them clean, gives them a sense or worth and responsibility which will help them as an adult desire the same sense of order.

The Master Bedroom

Finally, neating your own bedroom serves as an example to the children of your own desire to do as you teach. Taking the initiative and keeping your items picked up is the best beginning. Then a good dinner complete with a favorite dessert provides a suitable backdrop to approach another adult family member about your desire to solicit their help in keeping the bedroom neat, the clothes hung up, the dirty clothes in the hamper, newspapers, magazines and books on shelves, and miscellaneous necessities confined to "personal" baskets, boxes, or countertop trays.

When it looks messy, it looks dirty. More than half of getting the house to look clean is simply removing the clutter. Take a good look at your front room first, then approach the children's rooms, and finally, clean up your personal area.

Bathrooms

Bathrooms must be dealt with next for they are the rooms used most consistently by family members. It is best for each family member to be in charge of cleaning up after himself each and every time he uses the bathroom for any reason. Members who shower are to hang up their towels, put dirty clothes in the hamper, straighten the countertop items and wipe off the counter. When the toilet paper gets low, a new roll should be put out. When the mirror gets splattered with hair spray or hair oil, it should be wiped clean. If it is done each and every time someone uses the room, the bathroom also has a decent chance to remain orderly.

Setting a good example, keeping after offenders, and putting away some items yourself which consistently upset you but don't seem to bother your spouse if they are left out, is the beginning to an "uncluttered" house. It takes consistent, daily effort. Today, tomorrow, and each day for the rest of your life you will have to clean up your messes. If everyone helps, these small messes are cleaned up before they become mountains of mess.

Clutter, clutter, clutter

Lastly, it is important to understand there are three main kinds of clutter. They include:

- incoming (mail, children's school papers, newspapers, and magazines)
- rotating (dishes, laundry, clothes, shoes, coats)
- outgoing (packaging, produce trimmings, empty grocery containers)

All three need to be attacked, contained, and dealt with. For incoming clutter, each family member needs their own "in and out" tray, usually stacked one on top of the other in a convenient place in the family room. Into this tray goes mail and magazines which need reading, phone messages, and other stray papers found around the house which need a "home".

For rotating clutter, family standards need to be set as to when a job is "finished". When are the dishes done (i.e. they are in the cupboard, the sink has been scrubbed out, the used washcloth has been thrown down to the laundry)? When is the laundry done (i.e. everyone has put away their own clean clothes)? When are children's' rooms "cleaned up" (i.e. the curtains are open, the closet doors are shut, the bed is made, the toys are picked up, and the books are in their bookcase)? When is the piano practicing done (i.e. the piano lid has been put down, the music books have been put on the shelf, and the bench has been pushed in)? When is a child home from school (i.e. their backpack is in their bedroom, their coat is hung up, and papers for Mother have been retrieved for review)?

The biggest problem with handling outgoing clutter is two-fold. There usually are not large enough or plentiful enough wastebaskets to handle the garbage that is collected in the home during a single day. And, there is not someone reliable enough to get the wastebaskets emptied frequently enough to keep the stress level down. You know how it feels to have the kitchen wastebasket totally full just as you are beginning a meal and you have to take the time to empty it because "so and so" neglected their duty at the appointed time (whether it is your spouse, your children, or you). So make sure there are enough wastebaskets in every room. This helps encourage disposal of "outgoing" clutter. Also make sure the best worker is the wastebasket emptier. Doing this job regularly really keeps the house looking neat and clean.

Good luck! Remember a "decluttered" home almost looks like a clean home, and a clean home is a good place to live with and love a family.

COPING WITH CLUTTER Worksheet #4

Keys: <u>Cooperation</u> –   **Who?**   Person to Put Item Away

              <u>Convenience</u> –   **Where?**   Place to Put Item Away

              <u>Consistency</u> –   **When?**   Time to Put Item Away

Item?	Who?	Where?	When?
1.			
2.			
3.			
4.			
5.			
6.			
7.			
8.			
9.			
10.			

Chapter Six

KITCHEN ORGANIZATION

"80-20" rule: We use 80% of our possessions 20% of the time and 20% of our possessions 80% of the time."

SUPPLIES NEEDED: One kitchen

One large box for giveaways

One large wastebasket for discards

One sturdy box with a lid for kitchen items to be stored elsewhere

GOALS: Clear off the countertops

Clean out kitchen drawers and cupboards

Condense useful items by storing them together and within easy reach

Mary didn't like to cook. In face, she detested kitchens. Hers had the look of neglect and frustration which is often the case when things didn't start out right and went bad from there. The counters were covered with leftover banana peels, caked and dirty dishes, empty cracker boxes, and dry bread crumbs. The table had six meals of dishes on it. She indicated the family ate one meal, pushed the dirty dishes out of the way when they ate the second meal, and continued that practice until there were no more dishes in the cupboard. With this crisis, she usually filled both kitchen sinks with hot water and soaked all the dishes for an hour before attempting to wash them. She managed to get them dried and in the cupboard about three times a week. Then they would go on another marathon before she capitulated and did dishes again.

The kitchen floor was sticky and crunchy. There were dead flies in the window sill and a few live ones wandering around.

"I don't mind working," she said. "In fact, I work very hard to keep the laundry up, the mending done, and the front room cleaned up for company. But

the kitchen, well, it just is too much for me. He won't cook. I don't like to. The children aren't old enough to do it yet. How do I conquer this problem?"

Poor Mary. The answers seemed so simple to her once we talked about different methods and possibilities. She needed a jump start, a little cooperation from her husband, a printed grocery list, a Master Menu, and a timer (to set limits on how much time she spent cooking). Within two weeks she was calling me with good news.

"I finally did it," she said. "I fixed dinner before he got home from work."

"You should have seen the delight on his face when he walked in the door with the kitchen smelling of a fresh meal (instead of leftovers), saw the table had been set neatly, and the counters were wiped and clear."

"Actually, you should have heard the big kiss I got. Just that kiss gives me energy to do this over and over and over again, just for him."

Clear Off the Counter Tops

The kitchen is the central work area of a homemaker. Three organizational steps will enhance this work area and make it more useful.

First, clear all unnecessary tools, gadgets, and other "free loaders" off the counter tops. This instantly makes it easier to clean the counter top. Clearing off the countertops also increases the workspace and essentially gets you a bigger, better kitchen (at no cost). The question to ask is: "Is this tool a friend or a free loader?" Going from countertop to countertop, ask yourself if you use the tools stationed there every day. If not, it is usually better to store them convenient to the countertop but inside a cupboard than to leave them on the counter because it not only takes more energy to keep them clean if left on the counter top, but it also clutters your workspace and leaves one more thing to lift and wipe under when you are cleaning up after a meal.

Some items which are essential tools and current countertop residents might be just as accessible, but less burdensome, if they are replaced with the same tool which can be hung from under the upper cabinets. For example, hanging can openers keep the tool convenient and save counter space. Attachments to your heavy-duty mixer or your blender might be hung from the undersides of your upper cabinets. A hanging paper towel rack facilitates having more counter space. So ask yourself, "What can I hang?"

Other countertop residents might be kept in a cupboard above their current resting space. Drilling a medium-sized hole through the underside of an upper cupboard "floor" (or bottom shelf) would allow a hand mixer and/or the toaster to be kept easily accessible and convenient in an upper cupboard. The tool is kept on the bottom shelf of the cupboard, the cord threaded through the hole and plugged in the nearest outlet. When it is time to mix something, pull out the mixer, add the beaters and mix. The tool is already plugged in and ready to work. The same goes for the toaster. Open the cupboard door, pull out the toaster, place on the countertop, and begin. It also helps to have the toaster resting in a metal pan just larger than itself to catch those inevitable crumbs.

Other countertop residents might be kept in lower cupboard shelves. A blender which is rarely used, for instance, is better kept available but hidden for those occasional needs rather than hassled every time you need to wipe off the counter. The knife block might be given away and the few knives which you use regularly kept in a top drawer. Then there is one less item to clean and one more spot on your counter that is clear.

Sometimes, the counter is used by another family member who feels the countertop is the perfect resting place for keys, mail, coins and such. Designating a drawer for the treasures of this family member and putting these items into that drawer when they are "accidentally" left on the counter helps to keep the counter clean and eventually, you hope, promotes a new habit.

Remember, the countertops of the kitchen, whenever possible, should be kept bare and ready for the work the cook needs to do three times a day. Striving for clean countertops takes an initial decision-making process and then a constant vigil until other members of the family understand the countertop is a tool for the cook and not a convenient resting place for any and everything else.

Clean Out Kitchen Drawers and Cupboards

Second, clean out of the kitchen drawers and cupboards all items which do not directly relate to the function of the kitchen. The easiest way to do this is to open all the cupboard doors and drawers, mentally assess each cupboard's contents, and ask if those items really belong in the kitchen. So many times items migrate into the kitchen cupboards because it was the easiest place to put the item at the time. The question to ask is always, "Is this item useful enough to merit space in my kitchen? If so, where would it best be stored? If not, should I store is elsewhere? Should I give it away? Should I just discard it?"

After removing unwanted items, move functional, put infrequently-used items to the less accessible back, upper and lower portions of the kitchen cupboards and drawers. For instance, the turkey platter, the nicer holiday glasses and dishes might be stored very high and deep in your cupboards. Getting them out will be more of a hassle, but that hassle will come only occasionally.

Put your favorite, most-frequently used tools and food items in the front, more accessible parts of the cupboards and drawers. The best "friends" should be within reach 16" up or down from your elbow when your arm is resting at your side. Remember, the easier it is to reach, the faster your work will be done. Less-frequently used items are kept farther away. Really rarely-used items which still merit a place in your kitchen, are kept in places where you have to bend or stand on a chair to reach them. The question to ask is, "Where is the best place to put this item?"

Some items, like pans, need careful consideration. There are only four elements on the typical stove. Why do you keep so many pans and lids in your kitchen cupboards, usually far more than the four you might need to cook up even a fancy, complicated meal? One way to know which pans you really use, is to put all of them in a box and put the box in your bedroom. When you need a pan, retrieve it from the bedroom and use it. After a week, those pans still in your bedroom probably merit either a place in the hinder parts of the kitchen, a place in your storage room, or even a spot in your "give away" box.

Condense the Useful Items

The final project is to condense tools at the point of their first use. When you want to peel carrots, can you put the carrots in the sink and reach the peeler without moving your feet? When you want to stir the stew on the stove, can you reach a wooden spoon easily? Put kitchen sink tools near there. Put stove tools near the stove. Put cooking and baking tools near your mixing area.

Whenever possible, try not to nest your mixing bowls inside each other. Although it doesn't seem to take much time to unnest a bowl, the bowl you need always seems to be at the bottom of the stack. Try keeping fewer bowls "available" unnested and keep the extras nested but farther back in the cupboard. Then when you need to reach for a bowl, all you have to do is reach for it, a one-handed operation, versus the two-handed operation of unnesting.

In some instances, it might be necessary and prudent to have multiples of the same tool. Several sets of measuring spoons and cups, several rubber scrapers, several spatulas, for instance, keep the cook from having to wash a dirty tool just to finish preparing a meal.

Remember, a simple, uncomplicated kitchen works best. Discard or store elsewhere items which are not aiding your everyday cooking. You don't have to own all the gadgets, have all the cookbooks, and keep all those trinkets in your kitchen. Let someone else have the worry and work. Keep it simple! The attached list of **"Kitchen Essentials"** (**Worksheet #5**) is helpful in knowing what professional chefs consider most important in their kitchens. Maybe it would help you make good decisions, too.

So, first clear off your counters. Then clean out your cupboards, and finally, condense your tools, or in other words, put them where they will be most frequently used.

Good luck in your kitchen! Constantly be thinking of better and shorter ways to fix a meal. Every second saved is a second gained in physical energy, emotion reserves, and mental peace.

KITCHEN – Basic Essentials Worksheet #5

1 paring knife
1 serrated bread knife
1 10" chef's knife
1 kitchen scissors

timer
1 small wire whisk
1 large wire whisk

3 long-handled wooden spoons
1 long-handled slotted spoon
2 pancake turners (plastic)
2 spatulas (metal)

3 rubber scrapers
1 set tongs

3 sets measuring spoons
3 sets measuring cups
1 set glass measuring cups
     (1 cup, 2 cup, 4 cup)

3 oven-proof mixing bowls

1 fine-wire strainer

2 colanders

1 cutting board

1 small hand grater

1 vegetable peeler

1 can opener
1 bottle opener

1 wide-mouth funnel
1 narrow-mouth funnel

12 hot pads

2 9" pie plates
2 9" square cake pans
4 cookie sheets
2 muffin tins

2 cake cooling racks
1 rolling pin
1 candy thermometer

1 7" fry pan (with lid)
1 10" fry pan (with lid)
1 roasting pan and rack

1 1-quart casserole (with lid)
1 2-quart casserole (with lid)
1 5-quart casserole (with lid)

1 small sauce pan (1-1/2 quart)
1 medium sauce pan (2 quart)
1 large sauce pan (3-4 quart)
1 stew pot

Appliances

blender

crock pot

electric grill

electric hand mixer

electric knife

popcorn popper

heavy-duty mixer

toaster

waffle iron

Chapter Seven

FAMILY "INFORMATION" BINDER

"Having one place for all your important information will save time, time, time. Since we spend about 30% of our time looking for things, why not have just one place to look?"
Marie C. Ricks

SUPPLIES NEEDED:

One 2"-wide 8-1/2" x 11" 3-ring binder

Twenty or more 8-1/2" x 11" 3-ring binder dividers

One clear plastic, binder-size business card holder (for use as the Master Key Holder, behind the "Keys" divider)

Copies of **Worksheets:**
#7, Personal Information
#9, Safe Deposit Box
          Contents
#10, Personal Medical Info.
#11, Medical History
#12, Prescriptions
#13, Immunizations
#14, Childhood Diseases
#15, Maternity Record
#16, Dental History
#17, Special Occasions

GOALS:

Purchase supplies

Label the binder spine: "FAMILY INFORMATION"

Label the dividers: Family Members-Personal (label a **separate** divider for each member of your family, i.e. "Dad", "Mom", "Tom", & "Sue")

Family Members-Medical/Dental (label a **separate** divider for each member of your family, i.e. "Dad-Rx", "Mom-Rx", "Tom-Rx")

- Home

- Keys

- Miscellaneous

- Numbers

- Purse/Wallet Contents

- Safe Deposit Box

- Special Occasions

- Storage

- Vital Documents

Copy a "Personal Information" worksheet for each family member (see **Worksheet #7**) and put behind that family member's personal "Family Members" divider

Copy the "Personal Medical" information worksheet for each family member (see **Worksheet #10**) and put behind that family member's personal "Medical/Dental" divider

Copy several "Medical History" worksheets for each family member (see **Worksheet #11**) and put behind that family member's personal "Medical/Dental" divider

Copy the "Prescriptions" worksheet for each family member (see **Worksheet #12**) and put behind that family member's personal "Medical/Dental" divider

Copy the "Immunizations" worksheet for each family member (see **Worksheet #13**) and put behind that family member's personal "Medical/Dental" divider

Copy the "Childhood Diseases/Allergies" worksheet for each family member (see **Worksheet #14**) and put behind that family member's personal "Medical/Dental" divider

Copy the "Maternity Record" worksheet for each mother (**see Worksheet #15**) and put behind mother's personal "Medical/Dental" divider

Copy the "Dental Record" worksheet for each family member (see **Worksheet #16**) and put behind that family member's personal "Medical/Dental" divider

Copy several "Safe Deposit Box Contents" forms (see **Worksheet #9**) and put them behind the "Safe Deposit Box" divider

Copy twelve "Special Occasions" forms and put behind the "Special Occasions" divider (see **Worksheet #17**)

Complete the Family "Information" Binder by adding the necessary information to each of the sections

Carolyn was always looking for that missing piece of paper. She called me one morning in great frustration. She had just found the list of soccer practices the night before and already this morning the paper had disappeared from the frig door, again. She figured she was spending a good part of an hour every other day looking for some important piece of paper. Two days ago it was her husband's vacation schedule. Last week it had been the directions to the new piano teacher's home. The papers seemed to walk just out of sight when she was turned the other way. Actually, there were so many pieces of paper, flying in so many directions, she had no idea how to contain them all.

She need some help. After we talked a bit, she calmed down. It made sense, she said. Yes, she would try it..... and later that week she called again.

"It works," she said. "It works so well, I really should have thought of it myself."

Having just one place to keep important information will save time, time, time. A Family "Information" Binder is a 3-ring binder with dividers behind which important information is kept for easy retrieval.

<u>Family Members</u>

The <u>Family Members</u> section is prepared by labeling separate binder dividers for each family member in the front of the binder which allows an easy place to keep personal information, i.e. "Dad", "Mom", "Tom", & "Sue".

At the bottom of the personal information sheet under "My Wishing Well" is a convenient place to record "wishes" which family members may make. "I wish I had a larger plumbing wrench!" "I wish I had some blue knee-length socks." "I wish I had more coloring pencils." This special place to record a wish list aids in purchasing gifts at Christmas time, birthdays or other special occasions.

This is also a good place to keep your own wishes so you can easily tell anyone at any time what a good gift for you might be. Sometimes an advertisement three-hole punched and kept in this section helps define specifics. Since needed tools and desires are thought of at odd moments, having a special sheet to list these dreams helps to make them happen. It also helps to hint to spouses that this information is in the Family "Information" Binder. It never hurts to help "surprises" be both well-meaning and beneficial.

Behind each person's sheet, another blank sheet could hold clothing tags of favorite underwear, socks, and pajamas style and brands. Soccer schedules, piano recital dates, public school emergency plans, and other information sheets could also be kept here.

Keys

The <u>Keys</u> section is where a "master" copy of each important key is kept. A clear plastic, binder-size business card holder is the perfect tool for this. Put each "master" key in one of the business card holders with an attached blank business card upon which is written the type of key it is: house, beige van, blue truck, green luggage, etc. Then seal the pocket with a piece of tape. Now you have a copy of the important keys in your life in a safe place no matter what else may happen to your "working" keys.

Home

The <u>Home</u> section is a good place to keep exterior/interior house and trim paint types, brands, colors. Paint samples (popcycle sticks dipped in the paint, dried and kept in a 3-hole punched ziploc bag) and information about where the paint was last purchased aids when its time to touch up or repaint. Upholstery and linoleum samples can also be stored in a ziploc bag which has been three-hole punched. Branch, colors and style information would aid in replacing items as they wear out and in matching colors when decorating.

Medical/Dental

The Medical/Dental section might also have a divider for each member of the family, i.e. "Dad-Rx", "Mom-Rx", "Tom-Rx", and "Sue-Rx". The different medical/dental information worksheets help keep track of personal medical information, doctor's visits and instructions, prescriptions, immunizations, childhood illnesses/allergies, and dental work. While some of these information sheets will be used singly, others, such as the **"Medical History" Worksheet** will fill up and a second, third or fourth sheet will be needed for each family member as time passes. (See **Worksheets #10, Personal Medical Information; #11, Medical History; #12, Prescriptions; #13, Immunizations; #14, Childhood Diseases; #15, Maternity Record; and #16, Dental History**.)

Miscellaneous

The Miscellaneous section is for keeping all items for which there is no clear "home" but which need keeping. They include schedules for community activities, local athletic competitions, and cultural performances, and other printed information.

Numbers

The Numbers section is for credit card, library, social security, vehicle, license and key numbers. It is also the place to put down banking account numbers, the bank, branch, and addresses where funds are kept. Also, keeping the phone number to call if your credit cards are stolen saves much time and financial loss.

Purse/Wallet

The Purse/Wallet section is a list of all contents kept in the purse/wallet. This would aid recovery if the purse or wallet was ever stolen. The easiest way to record this information is to xerox all the cards (both front and back) you keep in your purse or wallet and put those papers in this section.

Safe Deposit Box

The Safe Deposit Box section should contain a list of items which are stored in the safe deposit box, the box's number, the box's location, and where the keys are kept. One key might be stored in the Family "Information" Binder but both keys ARE NOT to be kept together. (Use **Worksheet #9** to keep a record.)

Special Occasions

      One of the better ways to prepare for your future is to make up twelve "Special Occasions" forms (see **Worksheet #17**), one for each month of the year, and put in the Special Occasions section. List the birthdays and anniversaries of family members in pen for those dates you wish to remember for a long time. Make temporary notes in pencil about the birthdays of business associates, current neighbors, and your children's best friends so this information can be deleted later, if necessary. List the holidays you plan to celebrate. And then with the help of your spouse and/or family, decide how you will celebrate each of those occasions.

      For instance, Bob and Sheila liked to put the flag out on each national holiday so naturally that was included in the ""Preparations/Activities/Meals" column for each of those holidays. They liked to have a special meal out for just themselves as a couple on Valentines Day, their anniversary, and the Saturday night before Mother's Day. They liked to hike to the top of the nearby hill on the mornings of Memorial Day and the 4th of July. It was a tradition in their family to take each child out for breakfast on the morning of their birthday. They noted these special ways to celebrate on their "Special Occasions" forms.

      The "Special Occasions" section thus becomes useful when it comes time to make notes on this year's new calendar; it helps you remember just what has been done in the past, and what might be planned to do at this year's celebration. Preparing for upcoming celebrations is so much easier. Noting a new extended family's birthday becomes a breeze. Budgeting for each holiday also is possible because you know what you will need financially to make each holiday special.

Storage

      The Storage section is great if you use a storage area away from your home. It is helpful to keep a list of what is being stored, the agreement with the storage company, the address, hours and identification numbers needed to access the storage area. This section is also a good place to keep a record of the items which are stored in inaccessible areas of the garage. For instance, the blue trunk in the rafters of the garage comes down only occasionally. Recording what is kept inside saves getting the trunk down every time to "see" what it inside.

Vital Documents

The <u>Vital Documents</u> section could indicate where wills, marriage, birth, and death certificates are located, where social security cards are kept, and where insurance policies are located. Funeral information, the will's location, and a list of serial numbers and description of major purchases would also be vital. This is not the place to store these items; but this binder is the reference guide as to where documents can be found.

Other enhancements to the Family "Information" Binder include a perennial calendar and a conversion table.

To keep the Family "Information" Binder useful, an annual updating of the binder is merited. This is the time to discard unused or outdated information, review the different sections for correct information and add other types of information which have not yet found a "home".

The Family "Information" Binder can be as thin or thick as the family needs, but it becomes the best place to keep information important to the family.

If it would help this project along, my <u>Family Information Binder</u> has copies of information forms for a family of eight. See the rear of this handbook to order or visit **www.houseoforder.com** for more details.

Family members: Personal Information **(Worksheet #7)**
(a separate divider   School/work schedules
for each person)   Sports schedules

Home: Paint brand, color, type, sample
                         Upholstery samples
                         Flooring brand, color, type

Keys: One copy of all important keys

Medical/Dental: Personal Medical Information **(Worksheet #10)**
(another separate   Medical History **(Worksheet #11)**
divider for each   Prescriptions **(Worksheet #12)**
person)   Immunizations **(Worksheet #13)**
                         Childhood Diseases/Allergies **(Worksheet #14)**
                         Maternity Record **(Worksheet #15)**
                         Dental History **(Worksheet #16)**

Miscellaneous: Perennial calendar
                         Conversion tables

Numbers: Credit cards
                         Social security card numbers
                         VIN numbers, license plate numbers, key numbers
                         Description/serial number of major purchases
                         Bank account numbers, branch, address
                         "Lost/stolen" emergency phone numbers

Purse/Wallet Contents: List or photocopy all contents

Safe Deposit Box: List of contents, bank, box number, key number and
                         key location(s) **(Worksheet #9)**

Special Occasions: Twelve worksheets **(Worksheet #17)** with essential
                         information about holidays activities and preparations

Storage: Items, where stored and the date stored
                         Agreements for off-premises storage, address, hours
                         Storage unit number(s) and access code

Vital Documents: Location of will, birth/death/marriage certificates
                         Insurance policies names, company, numbers
                         Funeral preparation information

PERSONAL INFORMATION *Worksheet #7*

Name: _____

Dress size   _____   waist _____   length _____

Shirt size   _____   neck _____   sleeve _____

Pant size   _____   waist _____   inseam _____

Sock size   _____   _____   _____   _____

Shoe size   _____   _____   _____   _____

Preferred colors: _____   _____   _____

Preferred brands: _____   _____   _____

Important dates to remember: _____   _____   _____

     _____   _____   _____

     _____   _____   _____

School/work schedule: _____

_____

School/work address/phone no. _____

Wishing well: _____   _____   _____

     _____   _____   _____   _____

     _____   _____   _____   _____

     _____   _____

     _____   _____

     _____   _____

SAFE DEPOSIT BOX CHECKLIST Worksheet #8

What to keep in a Safe Deposit Box:

- ☐ ☐ Adoption papers
- ☐ ☐ Birth certificates
- ☐ ☐ Citizenship papers
- ☐ ☐ Contracts
- ☐ ☐ Custody papers
- ☐ ☐ Death certificates
- ☐ ☐ Deeds to property
- ☐ ☐ Family picture(s)
- ☐ ☐ Household inventory (CDs, photos, or video tape)
- ☐ ☐ Marriage certificate(s)
- ☐ ☐ Military discharge(s)
- ☐ ☐ Powers of Attorney
- ☐ ☐ Separation and divorce papers
- ☐ ☐ Social security cards
- ☐ ☐ Stock certificates
- ☐ ☐ Titles to automobiles
- ☐ ☐ Trusts
- ☐ ☐ Valuable jewelry
- ☐ ☐ Wills

SAFE DEPOSIT BOX CONTENTS Worksheet #9

Bank _____

Branch _____
Address _____

Key No. _____

Key #1 Location _____
Key #2 Location _____

Authorized Signers _____

Authorized Signers _____

Authorized Signers _____

Items in Box: _____ _____

_____ _____

_____ _____

_____ _____

_____ _____

_____ _____

_____ _____

_____ _____

_____ _____

_____ _____

_____ _____

_____ _____

Updated _____ _____ _____ _____ _____ _____

_____ _____ _____ _____ _____ _____

_____ _____ _____ _____ _____ _____

PERSONAL MEDICAL INFORMATION   Worksheet #10

Name: _____

Address: _____

Doctor: _____   Phone: _____

Insurance Co. _____   Account No. _____

Hospital: _____

Religious preference:_____

Dentist: _____   Phone: _____

In emergency notify:_____

Birth date: _____

Height: _____

Weight: _____

Eyes: _____

Hair: _____

Blood type: _____

Blood pressure: _____/_____

Past medical problems:_____
_____

Allergies: _____
_____

Medication(s) presently taken:_____
_____

Other: _____

Updated _____ _____ _____ _____ _____ _____ _____ _____
_____ _____ _____ _____ _____ _____ _____ _____

MEDICAL HISTORY Worksheet #11

Name:_____

Date	Doctor	Description
_____	_____	_____
_____	_____	_____
_____	_____	_____
_____	_____	_____
_____	_____	_____
_____	_____	_____
_____	_____	_____
_____	_____	_____
_____	_____	_____
_____	_____	_____
_____	_____	_____
_____	_____	_____
_____	_____	_____
_____	_____	_____
_____	_____	_____
_____	_____	_____
_____	_____	_____
_____	_____	_____
_____	_____	_____
_____	_____	_____
_____	_____	_____
_____	_____	_____
_____	_____	_____
_____	_____	_____
_____	_____	_____
_____	_____	_____

PRESCRIPTIONS Worksheet #12

Name:_____

Date	Doctor	Number	Reason	Type/Amount/Dosage

IMMUNIZATIONS Worksheet #13

Name:_____

Type	Date	Place
Chicken Pox	|_____	|_____
DPT #1	|_____	|_____
DPT #2	|_____	|_____
DPT #3	|_____	|_____
DPT Booster	|_____	|_____
DPT Booster	|_____	|_____
MMR #1	|_____	|_____
MMR #2	|_____	|_____
Polio #1	|_____	|_____
Polio #2	|_____	|_____
Polio #3	|_____	|_____
Polio #4	|_____	|_____
Polio #5	|_____	|_____
Hepatitis A1	|_____	|_____
Hepatitis A2	|_____	|_____
Hepatitis B1	|_____	|_____
Hepatitis B2	|_____	|_____
Hepatitis B3	|_____	|_____
Hepatitis B4	|_____	|_____
Tuberculin	|_____	|_____
Tuberculin	|_____	|_____
_____	|_____	|_____
_____	|_____	|_____
_____	|_____	|_____
_____	|_____	|_____

__CHILDHOOD DISEASES__ Worksheet #14

Name:_____

Type	Date	Symptoms
_____	_____	_____
_____	_____	_____
_____	_____	_____
_____	_____	_____
_____	_____	_____
_____	_____	_____
_____	_____	_____
_____	_____	_____

__ALLERGIES__

Name:_____

Type	Date	Symptoms
_____	_____	_____
_____	_____	_____
_____	_____	_____
_____	_____	_____
_____	_____	_____
_____	_____	_____
_____	_____	_____

MATERNITY RECORD Worksheet #15

Name:_____

Date of last menstrual period: _____   Weight: _____

Delivery date: _____   Weight: _____

Child's name: _____   Hospital: _____

Weight: _____   Length: _____   Blood Type: _____

Prenatal Visits:

Date	Doctor	Description
_____	_____	_____
_____	_____	_____
_____	_____	_____
_____	_____	_____
_____	_____	_____
_____	_____	_____
_____	_____	_____
_____	_____	_____
_____	_____	_____
_____	_____	_____
_____	_____	_____

Morning sickness: _____

_____

_____

Postpartum symptoms: _____

_____

_____

DENTAL HISTORY Worksheet #16

Name:_____

Date	Dentist	Description

SPECIAL OCCASIONS   Worksheet #17

Month:

	Birthdays	Holidays	Preparations/Activities/Meals
01			
02			
03			
04			
05			
06			
07			
08			
09			
10			
11			
12			
13			
14			
15			
16			
17			
18			
19			
20			
21			
22			
23			
24			
25			
26			
27			
28			
29			
30			
31			

Chapter Eight

TIME MANAGEMENT

"To fail to plan is to plan to fail."

SUPPLIES NEEDED: 30 copies of "Plan, Prepare, Do & Review" planning sheets (**Worksheet #18A**) if you are a "beginner" at time management and desire to carefully plan each day (this many worksheets will get you through one month)

Personal Planner: (for the more comfortable time management planner)

One 8-1/2" x 5-1/2" binder

50 sheets of 8-1/2" x 5-1/2" lined notepaper

Nine 8-1/2" x 5-1/2" binder dividers labeled:

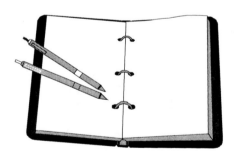

- This Week

- This Month

- This Year

- Next Year(s)

- Menus

- Errands

- Goals

- Thoughts

- Sources

GOALS: Purchase and collect supplies listed above

To prepare your personal planner:

- Xerox 30 copies of the daily "Plan, Prepare, Do and Review" sheets (**Worksheet #18B**) and put seven of them behind the planner divider labeled "This Week". Store the rest of the "Daily" sheets elsewhere. Write down tomorrow's commitments. Plan tomorrow's activities and goals. Plan the next seven days on Saturday of this week.

- Xerox 52 copies of the weekly planner sheets (**Worksheet #19**) and put four of them behind the planner divider labeled "This Month". Store the rest of the weekly sheets elsewhere. At the beginning of this next month, prepare four/five weekly planner sheets by adding the appropriate dates in the squares at the top of the sheet.

- Xerox 12 copies of the monthly planner sheets (**Worksheet #20**) and put them behind the "This Year" planner divider.

- Xerox 5 copies of the yearly planner sheets (**Worksheet #21**) and put them behind the "Next Year(s)" planner divider.

- Xerox 1 copy of the Master Menu planner form (**Worksheet #22**), cut in two, and put the two sheets behind the planner divider labeled "Menus".

- Xerox 12 copies of the "Sources" form (**Worksheet #23**) and put them behind the planner divider labeled "Sources".

Gloria knew she was working as hard as any mother and wife she knew. She was up early, she worked hard all day, she stayed up late trying to finish, but still she was frustrated and full anxiety. So much was left undone or half done. So many tasks were let go all together. She just couldn't see why others seemed so outwardly calm and in control and she was always feeling behind and frustrated.

"Take yesterday," she unloaded when she called. "Yesterday I went to the doctor's and sat there for an hour waiting. I could have been doing a dozen chores or running a dozen errands, but no, I had to sit there."

"Then when I got home I discovered the hamburger was still in the freezer because in my hurry to be done with my chores that morning, I had neglected to put it in the frig. And so we had corn flakes, again, for dinner."

"And, although I got the laundry started, it was still sitting in the washer when I got home so I had to dry it before I could give the kids their baths and get them ready for bed."

"And my children are always hearing, 'hurry', 'hurry', 'hurry' from me. Pretty soon they will think that is the only vocabulary word I know."

Working through life deliberately, being in charge (or at least feeling like she was), and responding to the inevitable interruptions were all challenges which Gloria had not yet conquered.

And so we visited. We talked about four principles. I suggested she try applying these principles, setting up a simple procedure to implement them, and then reporting back to me for the after three days about how it went.

The first day went much better than Gloria could have anticipated.

The second day she was ecstatic. "How could such a simple practice make such a difference?"

By day three she was exclaiming, "Why didn't I do this earlier?" And so Gloria was on her way....

Planning Tomorrow's Commitments

When you are learning a new skill, it is best to start small and simple. This is why I encourage first-time time managers to begin with the simpler project of planning one day at a time. Therefore, to get a good start on time management prepare one "Plan, Prepare, Do and Review" sheet (**Worksheet #18A**) noting the "timed" commitments, the chores, the meals, the phone calls, and other activities which need attention. For the person who has never used paper to plan, planning each day can be quite the experience. However, it simply means transferring all the commitments you have been keeping in your head, are stuck on the frig door, or are written on that small wall calendar to your planning sheet. It also means beginning to write down in one place things that need to be done in your life. We will discuss routine chore planning and regular maintenance in a later chapter discussing housecleaning (See **Chapter #15, "Housecleaning Plan"**). These items also become a part of your daily routine.

This simple, practical "Daily" sheet makes for easy planning. As commitments are made such as doctor appointments, picking children up from school, and evening meetings, they are listed in the appropriate column. Items which need attention but are not necessarily high priorities today are noted under the "Odds and Ends" column (odd jobs which need your attention some time). Three meals are decided upon and noted under the "Meals" column.

Each night before retiring, an effective homemaker prepares tomorrow's planning sheet by writing down what tomorrow will bring and making adjustments to suit the demands placed upon her. Items "to do" are done around scheduled appointments while some low-priority items may even need to be moved to a future day because of an unscheduled interruption. Food may need to be retrieved from the freezer in preparation for the evening meal, and errands could be scheduled around picking children up from school. All these ideas are noted on the "Daily" planning sheet.

It will be amazing how much more in control you will begin to feel. You will forget less, you will be more motivated. You will begin pacing yourself and gain confidence in your capabilities.

Planning the Week

After one week's trial of planning ahead day-by-day, it is time to begin a regular weekly planning. This is usually done on the weekend, say Saturday evening or Sunday morning. Seven more daily "Plan, Prepare, Do and Review" sheets (see **Worksheet #18A**) are prepared as above, and all the known upcoming events, chores, and items to be completed are listed for the whole next week. Dinners are also planned for the whole week. Each evening, the next day is reviewed and adjusted to meet any previously unforeseen demands upon your time. Planning on paper is an important key to having a better day.

When the beginning of the next month approaches, it is time to begin thinking farther and farther ahead. You have probably become somewhat proficient at planning day by day and on a weekly basis. Now it is time to get it all together. This involves preparing a planner.

PREPARING THE PLANNER

After purchasing the planner notebook, notebook paper and dividers, xerox copies of the appropriate worksheets, label the dividers as noted above, and put the dividers and worksheet copies in the binder.

First:
- Put seven daily "Plan, Prepare, Do & Review" worksheets (**Worksheet #18A**) behind the "This Week" divider.
- Put four "Weekly" worksheets (**Worksheet #19**) behind the "This Month" divider.
- Put twelve "Monthly" worksheets (**Worksheet #20**) behind the "This Year" divider.
- Put five "Yearly" worksheets (**Worksheet #21**) behind the "Next Year(s)" divider.

Preparing for Later

It is convenient to prepare five "Yearly" sheets (**Worksheet #21**) and just have them there in the planner. People will ask you questions, make remarks or talk about the future and you will now have a place to put down notes on paper. You will be surprised how nice it is to have someplace safe to make these notes so they are available for easy retrieval.

Preparing for the Year

The twelve "Monthly" worksheets (See **Worksheet #20** behind the "This Year" divider are similar to the "Yearly" worksheets above except that instead of showing one year they show a single month. One sheet is prepared for each upcoming month by crossing out all the "wrong" calendar configurations and leaving the right one. This monthly sheet allows space for noting birthdays, special events, and plenty of lines for making specific notes about times, places, and details.

At the beginning of the month, as you work through your plans, the information on the "Monthly" sheet is transferred to the four/five "weekly" sheets, spreading the items to be done to different weeks as is appropriate to the demands upon your time.

Preparing for the Month

As you prepare four "Weekly" sheets for the next month, each week's dates are entered in the squares at the top of the "weekly" worksheets (see **Worksheet #19**) and as appointments or commitments are made they are noted on the lines underneath the calendar squares. As you anticipate or plan for specific chores or repairs to be done, these items are entered. If something needs to be postponed and reconsidered at a future date, you now have a convenient way to write down items for future completion and not forget them.

When a commitment is made, circle the date in the calendar square so you will be cautious as you make further commitments on that date. For instance, on February 2, Jody's birthday party, you need extra time to wrap the present, time to arrange for a baby sitter, and a call to make to Jody's mother to make sure you have directions to the Smith's home. Thus, it would be wise to make Tuesday's schedule more flexible to allow for these extra activities.

Then, as you plan each week, the "Weekly" sheet information is transferred to the seven planner "Daily" sheets (see **Worksheet #18B**). This allows complete control to schedule items as is suitable.

Preparing for the Week

At the first of the week prepare seven "Plan, Prepare, Do & Review" sheets (**Worksheet #18A**). As you do, look at the commitments which this next week will bring and coordinate as much as possible errands, appointments, and other outside activities to minimize their disruption to your routine. Work through possible menus, ways to make the days go easier and times which might prove the best for certain activities. You will fill these sheets more and more as time passes and activities come to mind or are brought to your attention.

Preparing for Tomorrow

As you plan on paper for tomorrow, carefully look at what must be done, what you might like to do, and what can possibly wait. Select the order in which you will tackle your chores, when you will rest and make those phone calls, at what time you will stop your housework so you can fix lunch, and when you will sit down and read that article.

Think through all the possible ways the day might unfold and what you can do to prepare for all scenarios. For instance, I have learned to put any items that need to be taken with me on my errands right in the car, to get food out of the freezer first thing in the morning for use in the evening meal, and to walk through the day in my mind to see where I might forestall possible interruptions, challenges, or disasters.

Review the Day

The most neglected activity in a good homemaker's day is the short, few minutes near the end of the day when she looks back on the day to discern what might have been done better, what might have been left out, how she could have avoided that long line, how she might better encourage her daughter to be at the appointed pickup spot at the appointed time.

This reviewing of the day brings answers which will make tomorrow and the next week better and easier. Also important is looking for the things which went right. "Dr. Allen wasn't very busy this morning; maybe I should always set my dentist's appointments first thing to avoid waiting." "Gerald was calm in his car seat while we waited for Jessica to get out of piano lessons. Maybe I will always have a book or two handy for him to read in the car."

Menus- the Master Menu

Behind this divider a planner-sized copy of your **Master Menus** (Main Meals and Breakfast/Lunches) is kept (see **Worksheet #22**). This facilitates planning meals during the next week. These Master Menus are discussed in **Chapter #22, "Food Management"**.

The day-to-day menus which you plan on your "Daily" sheets can make the necessary adjustments to the Master Menu to accommodate leftovers in the frig, weekly grocery specials, and birthdays or other special events which will require adjustments to the Master Menu.

Errands

This section holds notes about errands that need to be run when you are out and about for other reasons. Write down the name of a store where you regularly shop, a certain mall you visit frequently, or an area of town where you occasionally travel. For instance, "Kohler's Variety Store", "Blossom Hill Mall", or "Porter City" might prompt you to write errands under these columns. As items are needed, they are listed on the sheets. Then when you are at the variety store, for instance, you can pick up these additional items without a special trip. It is often convenient to list size and brand name along with the item. On these sheets can also be noted directions, manager's name, store hours, and phone numbers.

Goals

This section is initially for preparing a short-term goal list (for the next month) indicating projects to begin, activities to complete and plans to consider. As you become more comfortable with goal-setting and completion, this section could also hold notes about longer-term goals.

What do you want to get done this month? Write it down, one project or goal per lined sheet of paper, and work through possible "short" activities and then schedule them in the "to do" area of your "Daily" sheets.

On your goal sheet you could detail:
- What needs to be done?
- When are you going to do it?
- Where will you do it?
- Who will help?
- What tools do you need?
- What supplies do you need to purchase?

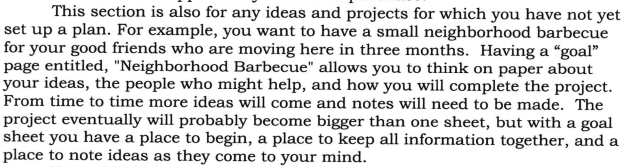

This section is also for any ideas and projects for which you have not yet set up a plan. For example, you want to have a small neighborhood barbecue for your good friends who are moving here in three months. Having a "goal" page entitled, "Neighborhood Barbecue" allows you to think on paper about your ideas, the people who might help, and how you will complete the project. From time to time more ideas will come and notes will need to be made. The project eventually will probably become bigger than one sheet, but with a goal sheet you have a place to begin, a place to keep all information together, and a place to note ideas as they come to your mind.

You might have a page which lists items to do in preparation for sending your daughter off to college, another page for good books you want to read, a third page for movies you want to see, or even a page for a large project like making a memory quilt for your grandmother's 75th birthday next year.

When we write down what is on our mind and begin to set down how to accomplish the task, we are more than half way done. There is now a secure place to record your ideas and plans.

Thoughts

This section should have several sheets of blank paper. It is used to record good quotes you might hear at a meeting or like when reading. It is also a place to write what is on your mind as you sort through life's difficulties and attempt to find answers. This section specifically allows you to ponder "on paper" what to do about your problems, how to deal with stresses, and where

58

you think you are going in life. You will often write down what is on your mind and only come to understanding as what to do about it with time and pondering. This is also a place to note impressions that come to your mind, lessons you learn, and diary notes you want to transfer later to your permanent journal.

Sources

This section holds information about sources, i.e. information you have learned about as you telephone different companies and inquire about their products, brochures which you may have received in the mail, or coupons you wish to save. The planner-sized "Sources" sheets may be xeroxed using **Worksheet #23**. When you to find the best rental car company to use for your upcoming vacation or a good source for bulk paper goods, you can now record the information easily and keep it for your later use.

Each prepared sheet saves time in the future because the information you have gathered can easily be referred to and used again and again. Thus, when you investigate the prices for landscaping trees, the sources for thermal underwear, or the addresses of used bookstores, you can keep this important information orderly and close by.

And so with time, patience, some preparation, and lots of practice, any homemaker can gain new skills, save lots of time, and feel much more in control by making use of a planner. She can look at her upcoming day with confidence, she can plan out her week with more flexibility, and she can gain a picture of the pressures for the upcoming month because it is all before her eyes, written down and ready to be organized and managed.

<u>PLAN</u> ... <u>PREPARE</u> ... <u>DO</u> ... & <u>REVIEW</u> !!! Full-Size, Worksheet #18A

<u>COMMITMENTS</u>

6 a.m. _____

7 _____

8 _____

9 _____

10 _____

11 _____

12 _____

1 p.m. _____

2 _____

3 _____

4 _____

5 _____

6 _____

7 _____

8 _____

9 _____

10 _____

<u>CHORES/TO DO</u>

_____

_____

_____

_____

_____

_____

_____

_____

_____

_____

_____

_____

_____

_____

_____

_____

_____

_____

<u>ODDS/ENDS</u>

_____

_____

_____

_____

_____

_____

_____

_____

_____

_____

_____

_____

_____

_____

_____

_____

_____

_____

<u>MEALS</u>

<u>Breakfast</u> _____

_____

<u>Lunch</u> _____

_____

<u>Dinner</u> _____

_____

_____

<u>PHONE CALLS</u>

_____

_____

_____

_____

_____

_____

_____

_____

_____

<u>THOUGHTS</u>

_____

_____

_____

_____

_____

_____

_____

_____

PLAN... PREPARE ... DO ... & REVIEW !!!
Planner Size, Worksheet #18B

COMMITMENTS

6 a.m.
7
8
9
10
11
12
1 p.m.
2
3
4
5
6
7
8
9

CHORES/TO DO

ODDS/ENDS

MEALS

Breakfast

Lunch

Dinner

PHONE CALLS

THOUGHTS

HOUSE OF ORDER – TIME MANAGEMENT
© Marie Calder Ricks/House of Order

PLAN... PREPARE ... DO ... & REVIEW !!!
Planner Size, Worksheet #18B

COMMITMENTS

6 a.m.
7
8
9
10
11
12
1 p.m.
2
3
4
5
6
7
8
9

CHORES/TO DO

ODDS/ENDS

MEALS

Breakfast

Lunch

Dinner

PHONE CALLS

THOUGHTS

HOUSE OF ORDER – TIME MANAGEMENT
© Marie Calder Ricks/House of Order

Month:

_____

_____

_____

_____

_____

_____

_____

_____

_____

Weekly Planner Form - Worksheet #19   © Marie Calder Ricks/House of Order

Month:

_____

_____

_____

_____

_____

_____

_____

_____

Weekly Planner Form - Worksheet #19   © Marie Calder Ricks/House of Order

Month:

_____

1	2	3	4	5	6	7
8	9	10	11	12	13	14
15	16	17	18	19	20	21
22	23	24	25	26	27	28
29	30	31				

	1	2	3	4	5	6
7	8	9	10	11	12	13
14	15	16	17	18	19	20
21	22	23	24	25	26	27
28	29	30	31			

		1	2	3	4	5
6	7	8	9	10	11	12
13	14	15	16	17	18	19
20	21	22	23	24	25	26
27	28	29	30	31		

			1	2	3	4
5	6	7	8	9	10	11
12	13	14	15	16	17	18
19	20	21	22	23	24	25
26	27	28	29	30	31	

	1	2	3			
4	5	6	7	8	9	10
11	12	13	14	15	16	17
18	19	20	21	22	23	24
25	26	27	28	29	30	31

31					1	2
3	4	5	6	7	8	9
10	11	12	13	14	15	16
17	18	19	20	21	22	23
24	25	26	27	28	29	30

30	31					1
2	3	4	5	6	7	8
9	10	11	12	13	14	15
16	17	18	19	20	21	22
23	24	25	26	27	28	29

_____
_____
_____
_____
_____
_____
_____
_____
_____

Monthly Planner Form - Worksheet #20   © Marie Calder Ricks/House of Order

Month:

_____

1	2	3	4	5	6	7
8	9	10	11	12	13	14
15	16	17	18	19	20	21
22	23	24	25	26	27	28
29	30	31				

	1	2	3	4	5	6
7	8	9	10	11	12	13
14	15	16	17	18	19	20
21	22	23	24	25	26	27
28	29	30	31			

		1	2	3	4	5
6	7	8	9	10	11	12
13	14	15	16	17	18	19
20	21	22	23	24	25	26
27	28	29	30	31		

			1	2	3	4
5	6	7	8	9	10	11
12	13	14	15	16	17	18
19	20	21	22	23	24	25
26	27	28	29	30	31	

	1	2	3			
4	5	6	7	8	9	10
11	12	13	14	15	16	17
18	19	20	21	22	23	24
25	26	27	28	29	30	31

31					1	2
3	4	5	6	7	8	9
10	11	12	13	14	15	16
17	18	19	20	21	22	23
24	25	26	27	28	29	30

30	31					1
2	3	4	5	6	7	8
9	10	11	12	13	14	15
16	17	18	19	20	21	22
23	24	25	26	27	28	29

_____
_____
_____
_____
_____
_____
_____
_____
_____

Monthly Planner Form - Worksheet #20   © Marie Calder Ricks/House of Order

Year: _____

January _____	July _____
_____	_____
February _____	August _____
_____	_____
March _____	September _____
_____	_____
April _____	October _____
_____	_____
May _____	November _____
_____	_____
June _____	December _____
_____	_____

Yearly Planner Form -Worksheet #21   © Marie Calder Ricks/House of Order

---

Year: _____

January _____	July _____
_____	_____
February _____	August _____
_____	_____
March _____	September _____
_____	_____
April _____	October _____
_____	_____
May _____	November _____
_____	_____
June _____	December _____
_____	_____

Yearly Planner Form -Worksheet #21   © Marie Calder Ricks/House of Order

Master Menu, Planner-Size

Name	Dinner	Bread	Vegetable	Fruit
Monday *Quick*	Pork & Bean Casserole	Honey Toast	Celery	Mand. Oranges
	Crescent Casserole			
	French Fry Burger Pie			
	Yakamish			
Tuesday *Mexican*	Soft Tacos	Cornbread	Corn	Peaches
	Chili & Chips			
	Enchiladas			
	Hard Tacos			
Wednesday *Poultry*	Oven Chicken Casserole	Biscuits	Carrots	Bananas
	Chicken Macaroni			
	Tuna Noodle			
	Luscious Lemon Chicken			
Thursday *Beef*	Porcupine Meatballs	Rolls	Beans	Pears
	Meatloaf/Rice			
	Primary Five-Hour Stew			
	No-Peek Casserole			
Friday *Italian*	Spaghetti	Bread Sticks	Salad	Pineapple
	Macaroni Beef			
	Lazy Day Lasagna			
	Mock Stroganoff			
Saturday *Easy*	Sloppy Joes	Fried Pears	Peas	Apples
	Hamburgers			
	Meatball Heroes			
	Chicken Gumbo Burgers			
Sunday *Breakfast for Dinner*	French Toast	- -	Carrots	Applesauce
	Hootenany	- -		
	Pancakes	- -		
	Waffles	- -		

Master Menu, Planner-Size   Worksheet #22

HOUSE OF ORDER – TIME MANAGEMENT
© Marie Calder Ricks/House of Order

65

Name	Breakfast	Lunch
Monday	Swedish Bread	Tuna Sandwiches
	Orange Juice	Carrots
	Milk	Milk
Tuesday	Cold Cereal	Peanut Butter/Jelly
	Grape Juice	Celery
	Milk	Milk
Wednesday	Swedish Bread	Egg Salad Sandwiches
	Orange Juice	Carrots
	Milk	Milk
Thursday	Cold Cereal	Bologna Sandwiches
	Grape Juice	Cucumbers
	Milk	Milk
Friday	Swedish Bread	Roast Beef Sandwiches
	Orange Juice	Carrots
	Milk	Chocolate Milk
Saturday	Granola	
	Raisins	
	Peanuts	
	Milk	
Sunday	Coffee Cake	
	French Puffs	
	Orange Julius Muffins	
	Bannack	

Master Menu, Planner-Size   Worksheet #22

HOUSE OF ORDER – TIME MANAGEMENT
© Marie Calder Ricks/House of Order

Category: Date:

Name: Phone:

Address:

Comments:

Name: Phone:

Address:

Comments:

Name: Phone:

Address:

Comments:

Category: Date:

Name: Phone:

Address:

Comments:

Name: Phone:

Address:

Comments:

Name: Phone:

Address:

Comments:

GOAL SETTING

"It must be born in mind that the tragedy of life doesn't lie in not reaching your goal. The tragedy lies in having no goal to reach.

"It isn't a calamity to die with dreams unfulfilled, but it is a calamity not to dream. It is not disgrace not to reach the stars, but it is a disgrace to have no stars to reach for."
                    Benjamin E. Mays

SUPPLIES NEEDED: Several xerox copies of **Worksheet #24, Goal Planning**

GOALS: Complete a "Goal Planning" worksheet for each project, large or small, which is before you (see **Worksheet #24**)

Valerie knew it just couldn't be that hard. She just wanted to paint the inside of her home. Her husband was being transferred in three months and the value of the home would be substantially increased if she could rid the walls of the crayon stains, the scuff marks, and the fingerprints. The painting needed to be done soon. But how could she find a whole week, morning until night, to be alone without interruptions to complete the job? And so she called me.

"Help," she implored. "I simply can't see a way to get this done. I don't have the money to hire a babysitter. I have other commitments, too, and my life seems so packed already with packing and preparing for the move. What should I do?"

So we talked of elephants and eating a spoonful at a time. We talked of taking the big and cutting it into the small. We discussed how many walls needed attention. She said fourteen. We found an hour every afternoon when the children at home could be occupied with a "video" or would be napping. We talked of how setting up and cleaning up takes more time than the actual project.

We decided on a trial. She would buy the paint. She would see how long it took to move the furniture away from a single wall, put masking tape along the baseboard and around the light switches, lay down the drop cloth, bring in the ladder, and open the paint can. She would paint carefully but diligently. I talked of keeping her supplies in a large plastic tote tray so cleanup and setup would go faster.

At the end of the first day, she called. "Well," she reported, "the set up took the longest today, mostly because I couldn't find the masking tape and didn't have a drop cloth that was long enough and had to find an old sheet to make up the rest of the length of the wall. But the painting went rather quickly and the cleanup wasn't so bad because once I had my supplies put away, I could wash up with the kids around and talking to me."

"I did it," she said in wonder. "I got one whole wall done today."

And so she continued. There were two days in the next three weeks when interruptions made her project go by the wayside, but the house was freshly painted in time for the transfer and she was delighted.

Just before they left town, she called.

"Getting the painting was possible after all. I just had to know how," she said. "Thanks so much."

Goal Planning

Setting goals is somewhat like looking down a funnel. The goals are at the large end of the funnel for your vision is often broad, non-specific, a bit untouchable and often seems unreachable. After the goals are determined, smaller, shorter and more easily comprehended specific activities are much like the smaller end of the funnel. They help you figure out how to proceed with all the distractions, interruptions and challenges that seem to keep you from your goals.

Day-to-day life throws us many curves including spousal stress (your spouse is home from work for the day unexpectedly), interruption stress (your son has medication he needs to take every four hours), emotional stress (a report must be done by tomorrow not next Monday), time stress (your daughter suddenly needs a ride to the play practice). How in the world can anything more be accomplished when there are constant adjustments to be made? Having a goal planning sheet really helps to identify goals, focus on helps and hindrances, and decide upon steps which are small enough to make it happen. We can learn to how to keep on track, survive distractions, and succeed.

Present Commitments

First, you must look at your present commitments. You can put up fences to keep the curves life tends to throw you from throwing you off course. You do this as you cope with your current situation, understand your priority commitments, and keep your goals in mind. It means saying "no" to some things in order to say "yes" to others. It always means hesitating before saying "yes" in order to make a valid evaluation of the situation. Usually, "That's a great idea, let me get back to you before making a commitment" helps give you time and space to figure out whether a new obligation, a "I can't do it now, but how about later" assurance, or "no" is in your own best long-term interest.

Your present commitments are like a circle-shaped "pie" which include personal, family/friends, career, church, hobby, community, "occasional" and "emergency" commitments. The pieces of pie bulge here and there with different situations. It is your objective to keep the bulges from becoming frigid in their distorted shape for long periods of time and, instead, pull them back into their proper perspective to meet your current goals. Other times, long-held dreams have to be put temporarily on hold for a period of time because other pressures and needs stand out and need greater attention. You cannot be everything to everyone all the time. There is no reason to be.

Saying no to someone might just be the kindest, nicest gift you could give them. It just might make them more independent, might make them look in other directions to solve their problems, and might help them appreciate what you have done in the past even more. Stop trying to run so hard! Catch your breath and with new order in your life do that which is most important first, that which is less important next, and let the rest crowd into the remaining moments.

Setting Goals

Second, you must look at the type and kind of goals you feel are investments in your future. You must meditate and evaluate frequently to make best usage of your time and corral the curves of life to keep yourself and your family focused on the best long-term goals. You will be busy for the rest of your life; it is important you are busy about the most important things first.

Most people can work on about one to three "extra" goals at one time. This means that in addition to their regular routine, pressures, work schedules, housecleaning, commitments, appointments, and responsibilities, they can reach out and above themselves in only one, two or maybe three directions. If you have not been really successful in making much change in your life, start with one goal. It must be a simple one, easily reduced to specific, day-to-day activities.

For instance, when a woman wants to be begin an exercise program, it is usually best to say, "I will walk alone around the block once after dinner" as a beginning activity rather than "I will arrange for a babysitter two times a week, drive to the gym, work out for an hour, drive back home, and return the babysitter to her home, take a shower and not expect any reverberations in the rest of my routine." Small first, bigger later (as circumstances allow) is always the best way to start.

Burps in our routines always cause setbacks and discouragement. For instance, the goal should not be "I will want around the block EVERY night after dinner" because that simply will not happen. It is more successful if you think "I will walk around the block on the week nights when my husband arrives home at a reasonable time. Otherwise, I will do ten touch-my-toes, ten swing-my-arms, and ten sit-ups before dinner on those nights when I know for sure I will not get my walk".

Some people say such simple beginnings get you no where. I beg to disagree. Any beginning, however small, is a better beginning than no beginning at all. It is the starting that is the worst part. Once you are started there is nothing to stop you. Nothing, that is, but a dirty diaper, a late spouse, a phone call, and a lot of other things. But keep it up. A brisk walk around the block, even a few times a week as you reach towards your goal of a better physique, will bring rewards far beyond the walk. You will learn to have a goal, set a specific activity with which to begin, and conquer the inertia which keeps you down and out.

Evaluation and Realignment

About once a month, it is important to stop for a bit and see where life is taking you. How is the "pie" of your life shaped right now? Is it too full? Is it misshapen? Where does change need to take place? The stopping and relooking is often the most important part of setting goals. "I set my goals too high." "I am not getting my family's cooperation." "I am working through the wrong activities to reach my goals under the current circumstances." "I need to change this and this and this." Sometimes just a small turn, a simple routine change, a short conversation seeking help will make the goals you have set and are determined to reach happen. Look, talk, evaluate and realign. You will get there. You now know how!

Step 1 WHAT IS MY GOAL?	
Step 2 PRESENT SITUATION:	
Step 3 WHO CAN HELP ME?	
Step 4 WHAT WILL HINDER ME?	
Step 5 HOW TO REACH GOAL:	

Well-written goals: - stated in terms of results

- achievable in definable and reasonable time
- specific as to expected results
- practical, possible, and feasible
- stated in terms of quantity, where applicable

Chapter Ten

CALENDARING

"It is not JUST to do more, but ALSO to
do better."
                    Marie C. Ricks

SUPPLIES NEEDED: One large, one-year, 12-page wall calendar (usually
                         17" x 22")

                         A different-colored marking pen for each family
                         member

GOALS: Fill in yearly calendar with birthdays, anniversaries, work holidays,
               school vacation and holidays, family vacation plans, and reunions
               (see **Worksheet #25, Calendaring**)

               Use this "family" calendar to note activities and to schedule
               projects on a monthly basis (use different colored stickers for piano
               lessons, soccer practice, and dancing lessons as reminders)

               Hold a family council each week to review plans, coordinate rides,
               consolidate errands, and organize household responsibilities which
               involve several family members (see **Chapter 11, Family
               Councils,** for further information. Use **"To Do Lists", Worksheet
               #26**, for younger children and **"Week on a Sheet", Worksheet
               #27**, for teenagers to help teach simple calendaring principles)

               Have each family member record their appointments and activities
               on the wall calendar with their "individually-selected" colored
               marking pen and as a family, review calendar each evening (maybe
               at dinnertime)

     *Patricia was frantic, well almost frantic. She had forgotten her mother-in-
law's birthday again. It came during the first week in March, and she hadn't
thought about it before the special day had passed. So she had purchased a
"make-up" gift, send it special delivery and also called her mother-in-law long
distance to apologize, none of which she could really afford financially let alone
emotionally because it had been a rough road from the start.*
     *When we saw each other at the grocery store, she came up and said, "I
have just got to get this part of my life in order. I am so tired of being late,*

72   © Marie Calder Ricks/House of Order

forgetting altogether, and ruining relations. I know there is a way to do it. Where do I start?"

I suggested she call the next day after she had purchased a large wall calendar. She did. It was already the first part of April, but never mind, I told her. It was better to get the rest of the year right, than to wait until January came around again.

We went through the names of all her immediate family members and added their birthdays to the calendar. We put a note on the last week of the month for all birthdays coming up within the first week of the next month. We went through extended family's birthdays, anniversaries, upcoming special occasions like the high school graduation for her nephew, the anniversary of her husband's big promotion, and her parent's thirtieth wedding celebration.

She made notes on the days when her children had piano lessons, her son had monthly cub scout pack meeting, her husband had basketball practice with his peers, and she was expected at the hairdresser's for the next haircut.

She had never written down so much on a calendar. When we were done, she was sick of it.

"I don't want to know my life is this complicated and so full of commitments," she complained. I told her it wasn't that bad. We had worked through the worst of it. If she still didn't like the idea after a month or so, she could call me and whine all she wanted.

She did call me about two months later. It was to congratulate herself. She had diligently referred to her "over-full" calendar on almost a daily basis and had seen her children look at it occasionally, too, in the past few weeks. When she seemed to forget something important that was coming up, they would remind her.

"Life seems to be going better", she exclaimed.

"Of course," she continued, "it was because you made me do so much thinking and writing down at the beginning."

"That's all right," I bounced back. "It works, doesn't it?"
"Yes, it really does. It really does."

Using a large wall calendar for family planning will save time, money, and exasperation. Purchasing a calendar and a different-colored marking pen for each member of the family is a good beginning. These calendars are usually available at stationary or office supply stores for a nominal price. The calendar could be hung on a wall in the family's main living area or near the kitchen table. The pens should be stored nearby. This makes the calendar easy to see, to review, and to use.

Noting all current commitments, known birthdays, anniversaries, school and work holidays, school vacations, the family vacation and any family reunions sets the parameters from which a family can discuss other activities. Updating the calendar once a month sets the tone for the month's priorities.

Athlete practices, musical lessons, and community and church commitments are noted as they are announced. Because the calendar is large, there is room to note times, locations, or other special reminders. Each school-aged and older family member is responsible for recording his or her own activities on the calendar with their individually-colored pen. Larger, fancy stickers might be used to denote children's birthdays and smaller, colored stickers might be used to note routine weekly events. For example, a green sticker on Wednesday means piano lessons are that day. Blue stickers on Tuesday and Thursdays means soccer practice is on that afternoon after school.

At the beginning of each week, a family council might be held when the calendar is checked to make sure it clearly shows all known family commitments, family work projects, and individual needs. (See **Chapter #11, Family Councils** for further details.) Coordination of rides, consolidation of errands, and cooperation among family members to make the best use of time is considered. Everyone knows what everyone else is doing and when. Nobody gets forgotten or left behind.

Plans can be put into place to prepare for birthday parties, call for restaurant reservations, and get gas in the vehicles. When the week is looked at carefully beforehand, it is much easier to anticipate and work through scenarios. This saves time and hassle. It makes for a smoother running family.

The wall calendar is also useful to note major cleaning projects which involve several members of the family. For instance, if the family garden needs to be prepared, it can be noted for Saturday. The question: "What are we going to do on Saturday?" has already been decided. When Saturday morning comes, everyone is more prepared and focused towards the family project at hand. Washing the windows together, cleaning out the garage and other major projects have already been scheduled so all family members can anticipate what the family is planning to do. It is also fun to schedule picnics, family outings, and shopping trips on the calendar since anticipation is a great deal of the fun.

Another hassle saver is listing what is being served for dinner at the bottom of each date's square. All mothers have heard the question late in the afternoon, "What are we having for dinner, Mom?" By noting the main dish on the calendar, the question answers itself after several gentle prods: "Remember, dear, I always put it on the calendar." Listing the menu also helps prod the cook to retrieve items from the freezer and prepare the meal in a timely manner.

When the family calendar is loaded with information, the family has one place to go to know what is happening and when. While it does take some time, effort and work to update, the family calendar is a tool which can help the family in so many ways.

CALENDARING   Worksheet #25

At the beginning of the year, put on your calendar:

- ☐ Anniversaries
- ☐ Birthdays
- ☐ Family holidays
- ☐ Family reunions
- ☐ National holidays   ☐ _____
- ☐ Proposed vacation(s)   ☐ _____
- ☐ School holidays   ☐ _____
- ☐ School vacation days   ☐ _____
- ☐ State holidays   ☐ _____

At the beginning of each month, put on your calendar:

- ☐ Appointments   ☐ _____
- ☐ Baby showers   ☐ _____
- ☐ Bridal showers   ☐ _____
- ☐ Commitments   ☐ _____
- ☐ Meetings   ☐ _____
- ☐ Family work projects   ☐ _____
- ☐ Piano lessons   ☐ _____
- ☐ Sport practices   ☐ _____
- ☐ Wedding receptions   ☐ _____

Chapter Eleven

FAMILY COUNCILS

"It is easier to work through future needs
beforehand than deal with the aftermath
of neglecting them."
Marie C. Ricks

SUPPLIES NEEDED: One large, one-year, 12-page wall calendar, usually
17" x 22" (See **Chapter #10, Calendaring,** for details.)

Several xerox copies of **Worksheet #26, "To Do" List,**
for use by younger children and **Worksheet #27,
"Week On a Sheet",** for use by teenagers

GOALS: Schedule and hold a weekly family council

*Anne felt a little panicky. She seventh child was soon due to be born and
she felt like she was losing control. Her older children were helpful with the
younger ones, her husband kept up his part of the household chores, but Anne
just couldn't keep in her head all the piano lessons, science projects, evening
commitments, homework assignments, spelling tests, and everything else that
was happening in the family's life.*

*She came to the first organization class a little befuddled and
overwhelmed. In the past she had been trying to be the family's secretary,
taking the blame when John got left at school for an extra half hour because she
had forgotten he had politely asked to be picked up at 3 p.m., feeling a fool when
Jason had to remind her to take him to soccer practice again, and wondering
where her head had gone when she remembered the piano books were home
just as she drove up to the piano teacher's home.*

*She was so pleased when we began to talk about family councils,
personal planners, 'family' wall calendars, "to do" lists for school-aged children,
"week-on-a-sheet"'s for teenagers and other tools to make life a little nicer.*

*She called me from the hospital after her seventh child, a son, was born
several months later. "I just wanted you to know I came to the hospital with my
personal planner. It has become like my right hand. We had family council over
the phone yesterday, me in the hospital bed and my family at home. We have
become so enthusiastic about coordinating our lives and successfully juggling the
events which are coming up that we didn't want to miss it even though I was
'gone'. It works, it really works. Thanks for making this baby's birth a joy. I
can't wait to go home. While I recuperate, the others will take up the slack and*

keep things organized and flowing. Everyone will feel like they are doing their share, and getting some of the benefits. For my part, I will just be glad to be home again. This time it will be a pleasant, more orderly place to go."

PRIVATE HUSBAND/WIFE COUNCIL

(A private husband/wife council allows the parents to work through issues privately so they are unified in front of their children. At times, it is even necessary to stop the public session of family council and regroup privately as parents so there is no tension between them in front of the children.)

Visit with your spouse about –

Scheduling the upcoming week:

- Commitments
    - To coordinate activities
    - To decide when babysitters will be hired
    - To decide who will be in charge of the children when
    - To know which children need to be driven where and when

- Family Chores
    - To coordinate any family projects that are planned
    - Work through preparations that may be necessary

- Issues
    - What conflicts between ourselves need addressing?
    - What conflicts between us and the kids need addressing?
    - What conflicts between the children need addressing?
    - How can these conflicts be resolved?
    - What will we do to implement change?

- Situations and/or challenges with the children
    - Which of the children have special needs?

- Situations and/or challenges with extended family commitments
    - Who in our extended family needs attention?
    - How will we meet their needs?
    - What should be done so we can keep our own family life intact and still meet larger commitments?
    - Who in our extended family is causing us problems?
    - How will we proceed?

PUBLIC SESSIONS AS A FAMILY

Preparations for Family Council

Have each elementary school age family member bring to this session of family council their "To Do" List from the previous week.

Have the teenagers bring their "Week on a Sheet" from the previous week.

The parents bring the "family" wall calendar to this session of family council. They also provide a new **"To Do" List** (see **Worksheet #26**) for the younger children and a new **"Week On a Sheet" (Worksheet #27)** for the teenagers.

Scheduling

Work through with each family member, starting with the oldest–
   Schedule for the upcoming week:

   - Commitments
      - Homework assignments and due date
      - Tests
      - Projects
   - Outside activities

Have each child report on assignments from last week's "To Do" List or "Week on a Sheet". (As a note, the "Week on a Sheet" can be folded into eight sections to fit easily into a pocket or purse.)

Have each child fill out a new "To Do" List or "Week on a Sheet" for the upcoming week listing:

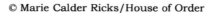

   - Homework assignments and upcoming tests (i.e. English paper due on Friday, Math test on Thursday with a reminder to finish these projects and study for these tests by the night before)

   - Extra-curricular commitments (with a reminder to make up brownies for Wednesday night's activity on Tuesday after school)

   - Chores which occur only on a specific day (i.e., taking the garbage can out to the street on Thursday night)

   - Work schedule (i.e., Monday, Wednesday, and Friday from 5 p.m. to 10 p.m. at the pizza parlor)

- Lessons (with a reminder to put the piano books in the car on Wednesday morning before they leave for school, etc.)

Have each children who can write, note on the family calendar (in his or her chosen colored pen) those dates and times when he or she will need transportation, when he or she has lessons, or when he or she will need to be driven to work and back.

Family Concerns

Children are each given a chance to express concerns regarding conflicts with siblings or their parents. This is not necessarily the time to resolve such conflicts and concerns, but simply a time to put them "on the table". After the parents have worked through the issues privately, they can unitedly, at a later time, address and resolve the issues with the children affected.

Children are also informed by the parents of extended family responsibilities during the week, such as family functions to attend or letters to write to older siblings and/or grandparents.

This is also an excellent time for parents to compliment each other and their children. In turn, each family member can find something nice to say about his parents and siblings.

PRIVATE SESSIONS WITH EACH CHILD

The third session of family council is between the father, mother and each child separately. The child is given a chance to privately discuss and complain about issues. He or she is asked about how life is going for them, where life is hard for them, and how the parents can help.

More than any other time, this regularly scheduled time alone with parents offers a time for the child to confidentially express himself and work through problems which are affecting life.

It is also a time for parents to generously praise the child in any way possible, helping him or her feel an important part of the family. Any progress is noted, and occasionally, as if necessary, discipline issues can be worked through.

LOVE at HOME

TO DO LIST

Worksheet #26

Sun	Mon	Tues	Wed	Thurs	Fri	Sat

TO DO LIST

Worksheet #26

Sun	Mon	Tues	Wed	Thurs	Fri	Sat

WEEK ON A SHEET

Worksheet #27

Sunday

8:00 _____
9:00 _____
10:00 _____
11:00 _____
12:00 _____
1:00 _____
2:00 _____
3:00 _____
4:00 _____
5:00 _____
6:00 _____
7:00 _____
8:00 _____
9:00 _____
10:00 _____
_____

Monday

8:00 _____
9:00 _____
10:00 _____
11:00 _____
12:00 _____
1:00 _____
2:00 _____
3:00 _____
4:00 _____
5:00 _____
6:00 _____
7:00 _____
8:00 _____
9:00 _____
10:00 _____
_____

Tuesday

8:00 _____
9:00 _____
10:00 _____
11:00 _____
12:00 _____
1:00 _____
2:00 _____
3:00 _____
4:00 _____
5:00 _____
6:00 _____
7:00 _____
8:00 _____
9:00 _____
10:00 _____
_____

Wednesday

8:00 _____
9:00 _____
10:00 _____
11:00 _____
12:00 _____
1:00 _____
2:00 _____
3:00 _____
4:00 _____
5:00 _____
6:00 _____
7:00 _____
8:00 _____
9:00 _____
10:00 _____
_____

Thursday

8:00 _____
9:00 _____
10:00 _____
11:00 _____
12:00 _____
1:00 _____
2:00 _____
3:00 _____
4:00 _____
5:00 _____
6:00 _____
7:00 _____
8:00 _____
9:00 _____
10:00 _____
_____

Friday

8:00 _____
9:00 _____
10:00 _____
11:00 _____
12:00 _____
1:00 _____
2:00 _____
3:00 _____
4:00 _____
5:00 _____
6:00 _____
7:00 _____
8:00 _____
9:00 _____
10:00 _____
_____

Saturday

8:00 _____
9:00 _____
10:00 _____
11:00 _____
12:00 _____
1:00 _____
2:00 _____
3:00 _____
4:00 _____
5:00 _____
6:00 _____
7:00 _____
8:00 _____
9:00 _____
10:00 _____
_____

To Do

_____
_____
_____
_____
_____
_____
_____
_____
_____
_____
_____
_____
_____
_____
_____
_____

HOUSE OF ORDER – FAMILY COUNCILS
© Marie Calder Ricks/House of Order

Chapter Twelve

LISTS

"The less you have to remember 'to remember', the freer your life will become."
Marie C. Ricks

SUPPLIES NEEDED:

3" x 5" card box (you can use the back part of the "Brain" Box to keep life simpler)

100 3" x 5" cards

Nine blank 3" x 5" card dividers labeled:

- Birth Announcements

- Birthdays/Anniversaries

- Christmas Cards

- Gifts Sent/Received

- Holidays/Special Events

- Picnic Needs

- Trip Needs

- Visitors

- Wedding Announcements

Note: In **Chapter 15, Housecleaning Plan,** other "Brain" Box projects are explained. The dividers and 3" x 5" cards from these other projects are usually kept in the front of the "Brain" Box.

GOALS: Birth Announcements - Prepare a 3" x 5" card listing names of those to whom you will send birth announcements

<u>Birthdays/Anniversaries</u> - Prepare a 3" x 5" card for each person's birthday and/or anniversary you wish to remember and file by date

<u>Christmas Cards</u> - Prepare a dated 3" x 5" card listing names of those to whom you will send Christmas cards

<u>Gifts Sent/Received</u> - Prepare dated 3" x 5" cards for those people to whom you regularly give presents to facilitate choosing your next gifts. Prepare dated 3" x 5" cards for those people from whom you regularly receive presents

<u>Holidays/Special Events</u> - Prepare a 3" x 5" card for the holiday and special event preparations you wish to remember in detail and file by date. These will act as comprehensive "instructions" cards as you prepare for holidays year to year

<u>Picnic Needs</u> - Prepare a 3" x 5" card listing items regularly needed for a picnic

<u>Trip Needs</u> - Prepare 3" x 5" cards listing items regularly needed for a long trip, items needed for an overnight stay at a hotel, and "things to do" prior to leaving your home for an extended period of time

<u>Visitors</u> - Prepare dated 3" x 5" cards for visitors listing: who came, what activities you were involved in, where you went, what meals you served, what the visitors seemed to particularly desire and like

<u>Wedding Announcements</u> - Prepare a 3" x 5" card for each person/family that is invited to the wedding you are hosting (cards are filed alphabetically and may be referred to again and again for future weddings)

"Why must I do something over and over again and still not get it right." It was Emily on the phone. Thanksgiving had just come and gone and it had been a flop. She couldn't find the pottery turkey platter and only remembered where she had put it AFTER Thanksgiving dinner was all said and done. She had bought the wrong kind of pickles again and her elderly Uncle Jared hadn't seemed too pleased. His wife had always had that special kind for him when she was alive. And too, the cranberry sauce had been forgotten until the last minute and her husband had to visit three stores before he found one that was open and had the jellied kind. What was she to do? Another Thanksgiving like this one would do her in!

Emily and I were good friends. We talked. We shared ideas. Then she applied the principles we talked about very readily. She began making lists, lots of lists. All of them on 3" x 5" cards, neating kept in a 3" x 5" card box. She made lists for what to buy at the grocery store a few days before Christmas, what to cook on the day before Christmas Eve, what to get out of the freezer on Christmas morning so it would be thawed in time for Christmas dinner. She made so many lists for that upcoming holiday I was afraid she had overdone it, but her cheerful voice on the phone after New Year's Day delighted me.

"It was great," she said. "I did just what we talked about. I know I overdid it, but not really. You can't really overdo 'lists'. I wrote down everything I knew I would need to be prepared for good holiday meals and then I let my brain worry about other things while I went cheerfully and confidently about fixing food and preparing for my company. It was so much better than Thanksgiving. Lists are the only way to keep it all together when you are stressed."

When a homemaker decides to get really organized, she will realize setting up a system for keeping records can serve her the rest of her life. Lists are kept on 3" x 5" cards because this allows for the greatest versatility. When bound notebooks are used, there is no flexibility, no chance to discard and add names and other information and still keep the whole organized and useful.

In addition, when we keep lists on 3" x 5" cards we can use them over and over again as the same event repeats itself in our lives. Additional notes are made as we learn from experience and make mistakes. The very act of writing down what we have learned keeps these mistakes from being repeated the next time.

Birth Announcements

When your next child is born, make up a list on a lined 3" x 5" card of all the people to whom you will send birth announcements. Their addresses need not be added to this list because your regular address file has this information. As the years pass and you have more children, this original list can be duplicated, updated and a new index card made for the next child. These cards is filed behind the <u>Birth Announcements</u> divider.

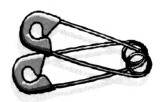

Birth Announcements

Baby: Thomas D.
Born: August 15, 20__
Sent Announcements: August 30, 20__

His parents, my parents
His grandmother, my step-grandfather
His brothers and sisters (4)
My brothers and sisters (7)
His aunts and uncles (8)
My aunts and uncles (4)

His work associates, my exercise group

Birthdays/Anniversaries

The 3" x 5" cards of birthdays and anniversaries are used to update your calendar every year. Therefore, they are handled a bit differently. Each important person in your life has their own separate card listing their name and birthday. Each couple has a card listing their anniversary. Notes may be added underneath regarding the person, his/her gift preferences, or other information which may be helpful when preparing for the special occasion.

These prepared cards are filed by calendar date in your 3" x 5" card box behind the Birthdays/Anniversaries divider. At the beginning of each year, the person or couple's names are transferred to the appropriate date on your large wall calendar for easy reference.

One important reminder: If a person's birthday comes on the first seven days of the month, a note on the previous month to aid in preparation can save much embarrassment because the birthday was forgotten until the new month arrives, and the card was sent late, or the present was not purchased and wrapped in time.

When you begin keeping track of nieces' and nephews' birthdays or those of other relatives you don't see often, it is often helpful to write the parents' names on the cards to avoid confusion. It can also prove helpful to indicate on the 3'" x 5" card what kind of card or gift was sent during a particular year (f one was sent).

<u>Smith, Andy</u> 05/05/98

(Parents: Matt and Mary Smith)

1 year old – card
2 years old – card
3 years old – card
4 years old – card
5 years old – card with $5.00
6 years old – card with $6.00

Christmas Cards

A list like that prepared for birth announcements usually suffices for Christmas cards. After each entry list the number of cards to prepare, i.e. "His brothers and sisters (4)". Again, the addresses are not put on the card because they may change from year to year. When certain people should no longer remain on your list, their names can be crossed out. Others can be added as new friends come into your life.

<u>Christmas Cards Sent 2---</u>

His parents, my parents
His grandmother, my step-grandfather
His brothers and sisters (4)
My brothers and sisters (7)
His aunts and uncles (8)
My aunts and uncles (4)

His work, my exercise group

Mr. and Mrs. B. Jones
Mr. and Mrs. J. Bell
Mr. and Mrs. K. Kelly
Mrs. J. Smith

Gifts Sent/Received

If your family regularly gives and receives gifts with other families, associates and friends, it is wise to keep track of not only what you give, but also what you received from year to year. This saves embarrassing duplication, keeps the value and kind of gifts more consistent from year to year, and allows you freedom to purchase multiple gifts (when they come on sale) and know to whom they have been given. A 3" x 5" card is prepared with the occasion, the name of the person or family, and the gift given or received.

Gifts Given

The B. Smith Family (Give on rotation every four years)

Christmas 2___ : "Monopoly" game, Special Edition

Christmas 2___ :

Christmas 2___ :

Christmas 2___ :

Christmas 2___ :

Gifts Received

The B. Smith Family (Receive on rotation every four years)

Christmas 2___: basketball, matching "family" gym shirts

Christmas 2___:

Christmas 2___:

Christmas 2___:

Christmas 2___:

Holidays/Special Events

Because traditions are so important to the fabric of a strong family, listing the essential activities, foods, and treats for each holiday facilitates remembering what has been done before and preparing for the upcoming event. There is often so much on our minds we forget where we have put the special decorations, what specific dessert Grandma likes at Thanksgiving and where to find those special pickles for Uncle Bob when he comes for dinner. The more information the cards contain, the more helpful they become.

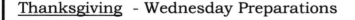

Thanksgiving - Tuesday Shopping List

turkey
dressing spice mix
mashed potatoes
gravy mix
cranberry sauce (don't forget – sauced not berry)
frozen corn
soda
dill pickles
bread and butter pickles (Uncle Joe likes Stein's)
pumpkin pie mix
pastry mix
frozen whipped topping
after-dinner mints (Dad likes Swedish green and pinks)

Thanksgiving - Wednesday Preparations

Make up rolls, bake, and freeze
Make up two pumpkin pies and refrigerate
Cut bread into cubes for dressing
Put soda in frig
Put pickles in frig
Put whipped topping in frig

Find linen tablecloth (hall closet, third drawer down)
Make up gumball turkeys as favors
Get extra chairs from storage area (in basement)
Change sheets in spare bedroom
Put out "company" towels

<u>Thanksgiving</u> - Thursday Preparations

Cook turkey
Make up dressing
Get rolls from freezer
Get margarine out of frig
Make up mashed potatoes
Make up gravy
Cut pies
Put condiments in dishes

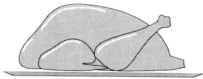

Set table
Get out Thanksgiving decorations
Put out turkey favors
Put extra rug by front door for wet shoes

<u>Picnic Needs</u>

Going on a picnic only to discover some essential utensil has been left home can be very frustrating to the hostess. One way to make sure each picnic is a success is to make up a list of what you need to take. This card is kept behind the <u>Picnic Needs</u> divider and is available to help you any-time you leave the house to have a meal somewhere else. It will save countless embarrassments and adequately prepare you for any mishap, especially with children. Notes can be added as you experience additional needs.

PICNIC NEEDS

Knives, forks, spoons   Hats
Bowls, plates, cups, napkins   Coats
Wet wash rag   Water bottles
Drink in thermos   Camera
Hot dish in thermos   Towels
Crackers/chips   "Collection" bags
Sandwiches   "Travel" bags for the car
Fruit/vegetables   Small shovel
Salt and pepper   Hand saw
Serving spoons   Binoculars
Dessert   Purse

Trip Needs

In the same way, having a list of items usually taken on trips will save the tremendous pressure of remembering everything needed each time you pack up the family. These cards usually are divided into columns to suit the needs for different occasions.

It is often helpful to have a separate card listing the items needed for the overnight bag for an overnight hotel stopover. This card lists the items the whole family needs to spend one night at a hotel. These items can be kept in one convenient suitcase to save unpacking the entire vehicle during a road trip.

TRIP NEEDS

Husband	Wife	Kids
Shaver	Pillow	Pillow
Driver license	Driver license	"Trip" bags
Credit card	Cash	Card games
Maps	Purse	Water bottles
Shirts	Blouses	Shirts/blouses
Pants	Skirts	Pants/skirts
Shoes	Shoes	Tennis shoes
Socks	Socks	Socks
Toothbrush, paste	Toothbrush	Toothbrush, paste
Deodorant	Deodorant	Comb/brush
Sunglasses	Sunglasses	Baseball caps
	Watch	

"HOTEL" SUITCASE

Husband	Wife	Kids
Toiletries	Toiletries	Toiletries
Underwear	Underwear	Underwear
Socks	Socks	Socks
Pajamas	Pajamas	Pajamas
Clean clothes	Clean clothes	Clean clothes
Alarm clock	Dirty clothes bag	Flashlights

Visitors

  If you live far from your family and friends and have occasional visits from them, it is a good idea to keep a short, concise record of their visit. This record might include the meals you served, the places you visited with them, and restaurants where you ate, and any special preferences they showed while you acted as hostess. Then, when they return you will know what to do again, what to avoid, and what activities will be new to them.

  It is also helpful to keep a simple record of the foods served and activities when you have a large crowd of visitors, say for a graduation celebration.

BOB AND MARY SMITH FAMILY'S VISIT

August, 20__

Served lasagna, fresh rolls, Italian dressing on salad greens, chocolate mint ice cream and chocolate cake.

Took their family to the zoo, ate lunch there.

Learned: Don't serve lasagna to young children. Have macaroni and cheese instead, then they will eat. Take wet wash cloth in Ziploc bag to zoo to clean up popcycles. Mary said she would really enjoy visiting zoo again. Bob indicated he also liked Thousand Island dressing.

PAUL'S HIGH SCHOOL GRADUATION PARTY

Served 50 people

Baked potatoes x 20, slices in half long ways
Hot chili
Shredded cheese
Sour cream
Chives
Plates, napkins, spoons, forks, cups
Lemon water
Soda pop
Sheet cake with "Congratulations, You Made It"
Candy

Wedding Announcements

A wedding announcement list is prepared a little differently. Not only do you want to list those you are inviting, you will want to make additional notes about those who were actually able to come, gifts received, thank you notes written, etc. This means a 3" x 5" divider is prepared for each wedding planned.

Behind this special divider, a separate 3" x 5" card is prepared for each guest. Remember, these cards will be useful for future weddings, both in your immediate family and extended family. When you prepare completely and competently for an event that is likely to repeat itself, the work done now is also helpful for all future events. Therefore, detailed notes offer a good way to keep track of all-important details. Other wedding information and papers such as reservations, receipts, lists of items to do, are best kept in a separate 3-ring binder.

HIS WEDDING

Invitation to Mr. and Mrs. J. Goodman

Mrs. Goodman invited to bridal shower, came

Received gift, thank you card done

Mr. and Mrs. Goodman invited to wedding reception, came

Received gift, thank card done

Conclusion

The lists you keep may also include other activities, special occasions or needs you may have. The important thing is you now have one place to keep all those lists, supplies ready to make up cards as needed, and a system to remember what you need to remember. This 3" x 5" card box is intended to let your brain worry about the other important things in life. Let this box keep track of as many details as possible to free up your mind and your life.

Chapter Thirteen

FINANCES

"One of us earns the money, and one of us saves it."
Marie C. Ricks

NEEDED: One 2"-wide 8-1/2" x 11" binder

10 binder dividers labeled:

- Budget Information

- Practice Budget

- Master Budget

- Monthly Budget

- Checking Account #1 Statements ("Fixed Expenses")

- Checking Account #2 Statements ("Occasional Expenses")

- Checking Account #3 Statements ("Variable Expenses")

- Saving Account Statements ("Long-term")

- Pay Stubs

- Paid Bills

100 sheets of 8-1/2" x 11" columnar paper with "three columns" (available at stationery and office supply stores)

25 sheets 8-1/2" x 11" cardstock (for filing paycheck stubs and paid bills taped neatly one above the other)

One 6" x 9", " 3-hole punched zippered pencil holder (for receipts)

Copy of vehicle(s) amortization schedule(s) (usually available from financial institution for a small fee)

Copy of home mortgage amortization schedule (usually available from financial institution for a small fee)

GOALS: Purchase supplies

Label the binder spine: "FINANCES"

Complete "Monthly Income" sheet (**Worksheet #28**) and file behind <u>Budget Information</u> divider

Complete "Fixed Expenses" sheets (**Worksheets #29, #30**) and file behind <u>Budget Information</u> divider

Complete "Occasional Expenses" sheets (**Worksheets #31, #32**) and file behind <u>Budget Information</u> divider

Complete "Variable Expenses" sheets (**Worksheets #33, #34**) and file behind <u>Budget Information</u> divider

Set up four bank accounts (or more) to allow for expedient handling of income and expenses (see **Worksheet #35**)

Prepare "Practice "Budget" sheets (**Worksheets #36, #37**) and file behind <u>Practice Budget</u> divider

Prepare formal, "Master Budget" sheets using columnar paper (see **Worksheets #38, #39**) and file behind <u>Master Budget</u> divider

Prepare long-term monthly budget sheets using columnar paper and file behind <u>Monthly Budget</u> divider

File paychecks, paid bills, receipts and bank statements in binder

Obtain amortization schedule(s) for outstanding vehicle and house loans and prepare a plan to downsize and eventually eliminate all personal debt (see **Worksheets #40, Debt Elimination - Example and Practice Sheet**, and **#41, Debt Elimination - Form**)

Purchase four-squares-per-inch graph paper and prepare a debt chart showing the smallest outstanding debt and go to work to eliminate it. Cross off one square for each dollar the debt is reduced. When this debt is eliminated, prepare a new chart for the next debt, and so on.

Jerry and Jo were in deep trouble. He had come into the marriage with some heavy debt and liberal spending habits. She had several unpaid credit card debts and no idea how to budget money. They "floated" with their credit cards for a while and were rudely awakened one day when their credit cards maxed out and they were left to live from pay check to pay check. When the ATM refused to function and the "demand" letters began to arrive from several creditors, they knew they were in trouble.

They met with me one night after class, waiting until all the other students left before they began sharing. They were out of money, out of luck, and their marriage was in deep trouble. Fighting over money night after night had created a tension in their relationship that had spread to other areas and was making them miserable.

There was little food in the house, few dollars to pay the upcoming utility bills, and they still couldn't decide where to begin, how to discipline themselves, and what measures to take to put a stop the unfolding tragedy.

And so we talked. They agreed to cut up all their credit cards but one (which they would use only for emergencies). They agreed to contact all their creditors and ask for a prolonged payment program to get them back on track. They finally agreed to mutual concurrence before buying anything that cost more than $50.00 (an discussion in which the truly deep tension between them came to the forefront). They agreed to sit down together and make up a simple budget of their monthly income and their minimum monthly expenses. We were to meet in one week.

After class the next week, they came up again. I could see there was still some tension between them but it was far less than before. They somewhat sheepishly laid before me their "budget", several handwritten pages of income and expenses which had been crossed out and corrected several times here and there. They had both initialed the budget at the bottom of each page and had signed it on the last page, a kind of "legal" contract between them that they would stick to this budget for the time being.

They had successfully disposed of their credit cards. Most of their creditors had accepted their plan for an extended payment period on their debts. They figured it would take them some four years to pay off their current debts using their current budget.

They were pleased and yet discouraged. No new "trinkets" or "toys" for four years.... Wow! It was almost more than they could comprehend. At the same time, it was a start and they could see a bit of light at the long end of the tunnel. Besides, they were going to work on this together. The first credit card had $67.08 due on it. At my suggestion, they made up a graph paper chart for their frig and went to work looking for more ways to save ....

I didn't see them again for about five years for they moved from the area soon afterwards and I lost track of them. When we visited again, they had gained two more children, drove a banged up car, and were beaming.

They had paid off ALL their debts, were now dealing with life in "real time" (i.e. paying cash or doing without), and had a new chart on the frig. This one was for a down payment on a condo, their next dream.

Economic Constancy

There are four principles of economic constancy. They are: 1) Live on less than you earn, 2) Distinguish between wants and needs, 3) Develop and live within a budget; and, 4) Be honest in all your financial affairs.

Live on Less Than You Earn

Live on less than you earn means that beginning next month you set the goal to spend less in that month than the income earned by your household during the previous month. Even if just one $1.00 is left, this discipline is essential to economic constancy. When you don't control your spending you will not have enough money no matter how much you make.

Thus, the first goal is to eventually gain enough savings to live on last month's money this month. That way you will never again need to worry about overspending.

It might prove useful to establish a money creed incorporating the following principles:

- If you can make it, don't buy it (which usually saves money and is fun besides),

- Don't spend money on that "which has no life" (in other words, invest wisely in tools and don't waste money on trinkets),

- Beware of impulse buying.

It is useful to establish family rules of buying. For instance, $10.00 can be spent by either spouse without consulting the other. $50.00 is never spent (except for weekly grocery store trips) without coming away from the store and thinking about it overnight. $100.00 is never spent without coming away from the store and educating yourself about:

- possible options (visiting other places of possible purchase where the item might be purchased for less and making a trip to the library to consult a "Consumer Reports" magazine),

- alternatives (will something else do just as well?),

- or denial (do we need this at all, can we wait for a sale, can we get it "used" later by watching the want ads?).

Distinguish Between Wants and Needs

It is hard to always understand just what is wanted and what is needed in a household for the needs and wants are both physical, emotional and sentimental. However, several skills really help make the decisions easier.

Usually, money spent for pleasure is money gone, while money invested in the future is money well-spent. In other words, always be thinking in terms of investment. That is why purchasing good tools are investments for they will serve for a long time, whereas eating pizza out is somewhat of a lost cause for a few hours later you start to get hungry again, no matter what you have eaten, and the money is gone forever.

When a couple sits down to plan out a yearly budget for holiday celebrations, birthday gifts, holiday gifts, and special occasions and then sticks to that budget, the affairs are less stressful because the family has agreed beforehand just how much an activity will cost. Besides, when you add up all the money you intend to spend during the next year just to celebrate, it might cause you to back away and wonder if there isn't a better way to "invest" your money and at the same time have a good time with family and friends.

Clothing purchases can be approached in the same way. With a budgeted amount agreed upon by the parents for purchases and further restrictions made as to time and place, the family is more relaxed because the temptation to impulse buy is overcome by the previous mutual decisions. It might be smart to schedule your clothing purchases: school clothes in the winter (for the next school year), new pajamas for everyone at Christmas, and summer clothes in the fall (for next summer).

Even then, three crucial questions help us to make good clothing purchases: Do we really need this? Do we have enough of this item already? Will a less expensive item do? Will anything terrible happen if we don't buy this? In other words, always err on the conservative side of less is more because more is a chore. More clothes is more work. It is much easier to care for, mend, and wear out a few pieces of clothing, especially for children.

Develop and Live Within A Budget

Develop and live within a budget. "Budget" is such a confining word when it is not understood and seems to loom as a restriction instead of liberation. However, a consistent budget, agreed upon by all parties and then stuck to diligently has more power to bring financial steadiness than about any other practice. When a couple decides and then goes forward unified, there is less stress in the family, more contentment between each other, and a greater capacity to have discipline when the "Jones" seem to be getting ahead. Remember, they may look like they are richer, but for the most part they are probably just getting more "in debt". Besides, having different goals than your neighbors isn't necessary bad; in fact, it may be very good for it allows independence and provident living as a family.

The "Finances" Binder

The "Finances" Binder is a tool for easily recording and reviewing financial information. Purchase the supplies as listed at the beginning of this chapter to prepare the "Finances" Binder. It has ten dividers. The first is for storing budget information you have collected. The second is for keeping the temporary, practice budgets which are used for three months.

Behind the third divider is kept the "Master Budget" for the year. The fourth divider is for the "Monthly Budget" sheets which reflect the income and outgo from each month.

The next four dividers are for storing the bank account statements for the different categories of the budget. This will be explained in detail later. The ninth and tenth dividers are for storing pay stubs and paid bills. The zipper pencil pouch may prove a reliable place to keep all the receipts from your expenditures. The receipts can quickly be reviewed in case a return needs to be made and can also serve as a reminder of where the money has gone during the year.

Budget Information

Setting up a budget first entails gathering the appropriate information about your income. (Use **Worksheet #28, Budget Information - Monthly Income.**) What have you earned in this last month? This last year? (Pay stubs and income tax forms will help immensely at this stage of budget planning.) What do you anticipate earning over the next year?

Where has the money gone during the past year? We can divide our expenditures into three categories: "fixed expenses", "occasional expenses" and "variable expenses". What monthly "fixed expenses" do you have? These expenses might include car payments, house payments, and school loans. (Use **Worksheet #29 and #30, Budget Information - Fixed Expenses.**)

What occasional expenses came up last year? (These are expenses which can be planned on but which are not paid out every month; for instance, property taxes, home insurance, car inspections and registrations, etc.) (Use **Worksheet #31 and #32, Budget Information - Occasional Expenses.**)

What variable expenses came up last year and will probably be part of your expenses in the upcoming year? (These are the unexpected expenses: a vehicle repair bill, a hospital deductible, or a household repair bill.) (Use **Worksheet #33 and #34, Budget Information - Variable Expenses.**) In other words, what do you anticipate will come in and from where? What do you anticipate going out and to whom?

Bank Accounts

Now it is time to set up bank accounts to anticipate and prepare for your goals. Initially, you will need four accounts (Checking Accounts #1, #2, #3, and a Savings Account). The first three accounts should have deposit slips and checks. The last account can be an interest-bearing account. (See **Worksheet #35, Bank Accounts**.)

The first account will be your "Fixed Expenses" account. All your monthly income is put into this account when you are paid. This account is called "Checking Account #1". The second account is an "Occasional Expenses" account. It is called "Checking Account #2". The third account is a "Variable Expenses" account which we will call "Checking Account #3". The fourth account a "Long-term" savings account.

This will allow you to deposit your monthly income into the "Fixed Expenses" account (Checking Account #1) and then write three checks to be deposited into your "Long-term" savings account, your "Occasional Expenses" account (Checking Account #2), and your "Variable Expenses" account (Checking Account #3). In other words, the first checks you write are to yourself. With time and expertise, it may be frugal to invest the sums in the "Long-term" savings account in higher interest bearing investments, but initially, just getting the money separated and put away is a big step towards discipline and accountability for you and your financial goals.

How Much Should I Save?

It is wise to put at least ten percent of your net income away monthly in your "long-term" savings account. Your goals will vary depending upon your family's makeup, but saving at least that much will not have major impact upon your lifestyle (after about three months of feeling like you will not survive this financial restriction at all) and still allow you to get ahead faster and more easily than any other type of investment. Just save 10% off the top for yourselves. There will always be a car to purchase, a house down payment to make, a marriage for which to prepare, education for the children needed, and your own retirement funds to be set aside. Saving early and small is a better investment than postponing and saving big later. The interest which may be earned from this account should be reinvested into it.

The "Occasional Expenses" and "Variable Expenses" accounts get their allotted money according to the "Master Budget" you will be setting up. You put these monies aside so they are safe until they are needed. Now you have a better "true" picture of how much money is left to pay for the rest of the "fixed expenses". When an "occasional" or "variable" expense comes up, money is taken from these accounts (Checking Accounts #2 and #3) as needed.

The "Fixed Expenses" account (Checking Account #1) acts as the main inflow and outflow money exchange. Income comes in, monies are disbursed to the other three accounts and allotted to specific "budget" categories within the budget and then reconciliation is made each week with a "husband-wife" review each month.

The Practice Budget

The budget itself is both a record of income and expenses and a regulator to keep you in line with your goals. At the beginning of next month it is suggested you and your spouse write up a practice budget (**Worksheets #36 and #37, Practice Budget**) with anticipated income and probable outgo. At the end of the month you meet again as a couple and discuss the reality of the income and outgo from the previous month. Look at where you fell short, did not use discipline as you had planned, erroneously under-projected or had unexpected extra funds. Then you write up a second monthly budget.

At this point, you try again to more nearly keep your expenses in line with your goals. After <u>three</u> months of regularly setting up a monthly budget (using **Worksheets #36 and #37, Practice Budget**) and reviewing it, you are ready to a prepare a "Master Budget" which will enable you to more formally approach your long-term budget needs.

The Master Budget

The detailed "Master Budget" anticipates not only the needs of the next month, but looks forward to expenses during the upcoming year, both "occasional" and "variable", as well as short-term and long-term goals. It is much more involved, because it looks at a whole year's needs, even to a lifetime of needs, and anticipates how to best plan and prepare for them. It also keeps more detailed track of expenses and income to maximize the use of your money.

The "Master Budget" spends all your anticipated monthly income on paper before it is spent in real time. Using three-columned columnar paper, first label the column "headers" at the top of each sheet. The wide left-hand column is for "Item". The first thin column is labeled "In", the second column labeled "Out", and the third column labeled "Balance". Then indicate monthly income sources (under "Item") and their amount under "In" with a total at the end of the list (under "Balance"). Then list, item by item, the categories where you plan to spend this money. See **Worksheets #38 and #39, Master Budget Categories,** for possible budget categories to consider.

First list the major "fixed" expenses, then the "long-term" savings, the "occasional" expenses, the "variable" expenses, and finally the rest of the "fixed expenses". Item after item is subtracted using a calculator and the balance left indicated (again under "Balance"). Most couples don't have any money left in their Master Budget by the time they have written down all the possible places to put it. If you do, create a category called "Fun Money". Remember, the maxim is to enjoy spending what little money you don't save.

The "Master Budget" serves as a guide and companion for the preparation of the formal monthly budget sheets. The first sheet of the "Monthly Budget" is the "Income Sheet" and lists, for real, the income which came in this last month. Then the income is "spent" as it is subtracted as a lump sum from this sheet and "given" to the rest of the budget sheets. These different sheets are prepared, <u>one sheet per category</u>, and represent the monies which will be spent and/or saved during the upcoming month. On these sheets the category goes at the top of the sheet. Immediately afterwards, in pencil goes the "budgeted amount" for this category which acts as a reminder of how much money to "give" to this account. The notes regarding how the money was spent and where is listed go under "Item" heading. When money is allocated to a particular category at the beginning of the month, it is listed under "In", when money is spent in this category it is listed under "Out". At the end of every budgeting session, the balance for that sheet is listed under "Balance". When a category sheet is used up, a fresh sheet can be inserted.

To help keep the budget updated, it is usually easiest to keep a check book register account of all expenditures both when you are away from the house (i.e. cash outlays, checks written, etc.), when you are paying for bills through automatic bill-pay or when you buy something by credit card (a real no-no when you are getting a budget started but which sometimes happen).

<u>Balancing the Budget</u>

Then, once a week, usually on Monday, the "fixed expenses" checkbook register is balanced against the budget. This means the entries in the checkbook register are recorded in the budget. The money spent at the grocery store is deducted from the "Food" category sheet, the money spent for the electricity bill is deducted from the "Electricity" sheet, and the money spent for shoes is deducted from the "Shoes" sheet. Each sheet is "balanced out", meaning money "In" and money "Out" are added and subtracted and a new balance calculated and recorded. All the sheets' balances are added together to form a "total balance". This is checked against the register balance and should match.

If it does not, something was not recorded, something was recorded wrong, or the figures were not added up right. Work through the issues until balancing is achieved. Weekly reconciliation of the "Fixed Expenses" account (Checking Account #1) keeps you on top of your finances. A monthly review of the "Occasional Expenses" account (Checking Account #2), the "Variable

Expenses" account (Checking Account #3), and the "Long-term" savings account is usually sufficient because fewer checks are written from these latter three accounts.

Monthly Review as a Couple

A monthly review with your spouse keeps both of you up-to-date and unified about past expenditures, anticipated expenses, and goals. Ask yourself such questions as: Where have we been? Where are we planning to go? How will we save? How will we spend?

Why go to this much work? Because being your own financial advisor is about the best financial investment you can make. If you don't watch over your money with care, who will? If you do, there is no end to the goals you can work towards together to achieve economic constancy.

Debt Reduction and Elimination

Now to face the really difficult financial demon: Debt. Where do you start and how to you best make progress? The answers are simple, a bit more difficult to implement, and very satisfying once they are achieved. When the money you would have paid others in interest is yours to use at your discretion and for your own needs, you are on the road to financial prosperity.

An interesting quote indicates: "There are only two types of people who deal in interest -- those who understand it and those who do not understand it. Those who understand it, collect it. Those who do not understand it, pay it." (from the Church News Section, "Deseret News", 1/9/93)

Most families have several different kinds of debts. These might include consumer debt, educational debt, vehicle debt and a house mortgage. When the determination is made to get out of debt, the easiest place to start is to take all but one credit card (which card is kept for emergencies), and cut them up. This is the best form of plastic surgery. However, if your spouse is absolutely against such a drastic plan, place the credit cards in a plastic container, fill the container with water and freeze it. From now on, all new purchases must be made within the parameters of the budget you have set up. Except for true emergencies, all purchases are saved for before they are purchased with cash. You truly become cash buyers. If you can't afford it, you don't buy it. Buying on time is bad financial policy for the habits of enjoying the pleasure without paying the price makes for erroneous and warped financial perspectives. It almost always is the road to financial stress and possible financial ruin.

Paying Off Consumer Debts

Now, make a list of all your debtors and the money owed to each. (See **Worksheet #40, Debt Elimination - Example and Practice Sheet,** and **Worksheet #41, Debt Elimination - Form**.) Work through a plan to eliminate your consumer debt beginning with the smallest debt and working towards the largest.

Focusing first on the smallest debt, prepare a chart of the outstanding amount on the purchased graph paper. Remember, each square represents one dollar in debt. Outline the number of squares which represents this debt. This chart is posted in a prominent place in your home (such as the refrigerator) to remind all family members the current financial goal is to reduce this debt completely. Such a charts not only acts as a reminder but also helps when making a decision such as, "Shall we go out for pizza tonight?" $20.00 not spent on pizza is $20.00 which can be used to reduce the debt. Every time a dollar is saved and put towards the debt, a square on the chart is crossed off.

Continue to make monthly payments on all debts as you have been doing before, but put every extra penny, nickel, dime and dollar towards your family's financial goal. Remember it took some time to get into debt. It will take patience and diligence to get out again.

Once the smallest debt is gone, the next larger debt is chosen, a chart made up, family cooperation solicited, and off you run again. Debt servicing money used for the smallest debt can now be used to pay off the second debt and so on. Each subsequent success in eliminating a debt brings your family closer to financial security.

For some couples, the consumer debts are so many and so large that professional help is needed to manage the debt before it can be reduced. Many cities and counties have consumer credit counseling services provided by governmental agencies. Usually for a small fee, these services provide counseling, help in dealing with creditors, and implement plans for managing consumer debt and then reducing and eliminating it.

Paying Off Vehicle Debts

Once you have conquered your credit card debt, the next step is usually vehicle debt. This is a bit more involved because there is usually a loan with a fixed amount, a fixed timetable, and lots of interest. Contact the financial institution which holds your loan and ask for an amortization schedule. This schedule lists the monthly payment which you make, how the payment is divided between interest and principal, and how many months are left on the loan. Once this schedule is in hand, it is easy to get motivated to pay not only the monthly payment, but the next month's principal payment, which reduces the loan by that same month's interest payment.

Again, make up a graph paper chart outlining the number of squares representing the outstanding vehicle debt. Cross off the squares any time money is put towards the car loan. It is surprising how much easier it is to "save" when there is a specific reason to do so.

It is helpful to contact a specific person at the financial institution with which to make regular principal reductions on the loan. There is usually a very particular way to make the payment, a specific office to send it to, and it is wise to check up after the payment is received to make sure it was entered as a principal reduction on the loan. Putting all extra funds from the monthly budget towards paying off your vehicle loan is usually a far better investment than keeping it in a savings account which may earn the same or less interest than you are spending on that car loan.

Once the vehicle loan is paid off, set up a savings account for your next vehicle. Each month put aside the amount of money you were putting towards the vehicle payment into this savings account and try to get your car to go and go and go until you have enough cash for the next vehicle purchase. Sometimes this money must be used for vehicle repairs, but it is usually sound advice to keep a car as long as possible versus trading it in for a new car. This way there is no new car loan, insurance rates are cheaper and you are definitely pulling away from the "Jones" all together.

Emergency Cash

It has previously been suggested 10% of your net income be put away every month in a long-term savings account. This account serves as your "emergency cash" account until you are able to pay off your consumer and vehicle debts.

When these debts have been eliminated, it is time to establish a formal "emergency cash" account for potential emergencies. It is suggested that three to six month's living expenses be set aside as prudent preparation. This means figuring what is the least amount you could live on for three to six months in an emergency and then making up a graph paper chart with this goal in mind. Every month put away as much as you can towards this goal. The habits of thrift and savings which you are establishing will bless your life and also bring security to your future. You can afford to be "cheap" now because you are investing in yourself and your family. You are reaching towards financial stability and safety.

Once this goal has been met, have a big celebration. You are ready for the final, hardest, longest and most joyful financial reduction journey. It will be worth every step, but it will take focus and restraint all along the way.

Home Mortgage Elimination

The last and most important goal is to completely eliminate all debt from your life. This usually means tackling the home mortgage. The first step is to arrange for a copy of your home mortgage amortization schedule. This schedule will detail the amount of your monthly payment and indicate how much is going towards interest and what amount goes to reduce your loan each month.

This schedule provides motivation in two ways. First, most home mortgages are constructed such that the longer you pay on the loan the higher the percentage of the monthly payment that goes towards the debt reduction. This means that each succeeding month you pay down on your loan, you are actually gaining more debt reduction per dollar "invested". Second, each time you are able to pay off the "principal" reduction for the next month you automatically are saving the "interest" for that month. (Although you don't ever see that money, neither will it ever have to be paid on the loan).

It is valuable to have both the amortization schedule and a graph paper chart. This time it might be wise to have each square represent $10.00. Otherwise, you might be able to wallpaper your kitchen with graph paper. Each and every $1.00 that can be saved is put towards this important goal. This includes the unneeded "consumer debt servicing money", your bonuses, cash gifts, and unused budget amounts each month.

As you get excited about this project, it is possible to reduce and reduce again the amount of money you need to live on. Suddenly and quite permanently, you don't "want" so many things which you were previously sure you "needed". Knowing that one extra monthly payment a year can knock substantial interest off a fixed thirty-year loan is plenty of motivation to skip the small pleasures temporarily for the larger goal. Doubling principal payments can almost reduce the length of the loan by half. Each and every time you put away money towards this goal, it is likely the best investment you could be making towards your own future.

Sometimes couples get very discouraged up front because the loan seems so large and their capacity to save so meager, but don't give up. Surprisingly, it is more fun to save than to spend, especially when you look around at your neighbors and realize that all most are doing is getting deeper and deeper in debt. You are climbing up. They are sliding down. Some day, some day sooner than you might think, you will be out of debt. It is a freedom well worth waiting for and working towards.

One project that helps is to set "mini" goals. Try one month to put away one-half of next month's principal. Or, try to put away three months' principal in the next four months. Or, try to reduce the loan by 1% by Christmas.

When that magic day comes when you are able to rid yourselves of completely of debt, you may want to consider having a new family holiday. You might want to call it "Freedom Day", a personal celebration of you and your family's discipline to walk a difficult road to the end. Now there will be new challenges, new expenses, and maybe even new temptations to return to debt.

But it is doubtful, after such a long climb out of debt that you will readily return to old places so quickly. Encourage your friends with your own experiences and attempt to remain financially "free" for the rest of your life.

Be Honest in Your Financial Affairs

The most important financial principle is being completely honest with yourself. Then you must always, always be honest in all your financial dealing with others. Doing so will bring a good night's sleep, the ability to look at yourself in the mirror, and the wisdom to deal with financial stresses logically and strategically. Neither you nor anyone else will ever wonder or worry quite as much if in all your affairs you are honest. This honesty is imperative as you look at purchases and make decisions which will affect your future.

So now you have the keys to financial stability and economic constancy. Work hard but never spend more than you earn, invest consistently by thinking tools not trinkets, always have a budget that works for you, set goals to get out of debt, and be completely honest. Good luck! And remember, the road is hard, long and uphill, but it is, nevertheless the best road to climb to the end.

BUDGET INFORMATION Worksheet #28

Monthly Income   From _____ to _____

Regular take-home pay $_____

Spouse's take-home pay $_____

Bonuses $_____

Tips $_____

Interest Income $_____

Other $_____

Other $_____

Other $_____

Total $_____

Yearly Income   From _____ to _____

Regular take-home pay $_____

Spouse's take-home pay $_____

Bonuses $_____

Tips $_____

Interest Income $_____

Dividend Income $_____

Other $_____

Other $_____

Other $_____

Total $_____

BUDGET INFORMATION Worksheet #29

	Past Month _____	Past Year _____
Fixed Expenses (items paid each month)		
Car payment	$_____	$_____
Car payment	$_____	$_____
Credit card payment	$_____	$_____
Credit card payment	$_____	$_____
Church/charity contributions	$_____	$_____
Dental Insurance	$_____	$_____
House payment/rent	$_____	$_____
Medical insurance	$_____	$_____
Other loan payment(s)	$_____	$_____
Other loan payment(s)	$_____	$_____
Occasional expenses (to #2 account) (See **Worksheets #31 and #32**)	$_____	$_____
Variable expenses (to #3 account) (See **Worksheets #33 and #34**)	$_____	$_____
Long-term savings (to savings acct.)	$_____	$_____

* *

Allowance	$_____	$_____
Child care	$_____	$_____
Clothing	$_____	$_____
Diapers	$_____	$_____
Electricity	$_____	$_____
Food - groceries – week 1	$_____	$_____
- groceries – week 2	$_____	$_____
- groceries – week 3	$_____	$_____
- groceries – week 4	$_____	$_____
- dinner out	$_____	$_____

BUDGET INFORMATION (continued)   Worksheet #30

Fixed Expenses (continued) (items paid each month)	Past Month _____	Past Year _____
Garbage	$_____	$_____
Gasoline	$_____	$_____
Haircuts	$_____	$_____
Natural gas	$_____	$_____
Newspaper	$_____	$_____
Phone	$_____	$_____
Pocket money	$_____	$_____
Recreation	$_____	$_____
Sewer	$_____	$_____
Shoes	$_____	$_____
Variety (non-food items)	$_____	$_____
Water	$_____	$_____
Other	$_____	$_____
Other	$_____	$_____
Other	$_____	$_____
Other	$_____	$_____
Other	$_____	$_____
Total	$_____	$_____

BUDGET INFORMATION   Worksheet #31

Occasional Expenses
(less frequently then monthly, but paid on a regular basis throughout the year)

	Month(s) Paid:	Amount:
Car insurance	_____	$_____
Car registration	_____	$_____
Christmas	_____	$_____
Dentist #1	_____	$_____
Dentist #2	_____	$_____
Food storage #1 (food items)	_____	$_____
Food storage #2 (food items)	_____	$_____
Holidays	_____	$_____
Home insurance	_____	$_____
Home storage (non-food items)	_____	$_____
Internet service	_____	$_____
Life insurance	_____	$_____
Magazines	_____	$_____
Professional dues	_____	$_____
Property taxes	_____	$_____
Smog/safety vehicle inspection	_____	$_____
Summer recreation	_____	$_____
Vacation	_____	$_____

BUDGET INFORMATION (continued)

Occasional Expenses (continued)
(less frequently then monthly,
but paid on a regular basis
throughout the year)

	Month(s) Paid:	Amount:
Other _____	_____	$_____
Other _____	_____	$_____
Other _____	_____	$_____
Other _____	_____	$_____
Other _____	_____	$_____
Other _____	_____	$_____
Other _____	_____	$_____
Other _____	_____	$_____
Total		$_____

Total $ _____ + 10% @ $ _____ = $_____ ./. by 12 = $ _____

BUDGET INFORMATION Worksheet #33

Variable Expenses (who knows when, but it is sure to happen)	Spent last year:	Amount to save:
Birthdays (gifts, parties)	$_____	$_____
Car maintenance	$_____	$_____
Car repair	$_____	$_____
Checks	$_____	$_____
Dry cleaning	$_____	$_____
Film (processing, prints)	$_____	$_____
Furnace filters	$_____	$_____
Home maintenance	$_____	$_____
Home repairs	$_____	$_____
Office (gifts, meals out)	$_____	$_____
Orthodontist	$_____	$_____
Prescriptions	$_____	$_____
Repair – long term needs	$_____	$_____
Repair – short term needs	$_____	$_____
School (fees, pictures, etc.)	$_____	$_____
Scouts (registration, uniform, etc.)	$_____	$_____
Sports (equipment, uniform, etc.)	$_____	$_____
Stamps	$_____	$_____
Tires	$_____	$_____

BUDGET INFORMATION (continued) Worksheet #34

Variable Expenses (continued) (who knows when, but it is sure to happen)	Spent last year:	Amount to save:
Yard (plants, supplies, etc.)	$_____	$_____
Other	$_____	$_____
Other	$_____	$_____
Other	$_____	$_____
Other	$_____	$_____
Other	$_____	$_____
Other	$_____	$_____
Total	$_____	$_____

Total $ _____ + 10% @ $ _____ = $_____ ./. by 12 = $ _____

BANK ACCOUNTS Worksheet #35

Set up bank accounts to meet your needs
using the following suggestions.

Then divide and deposit your income
into the appropriate accounts.

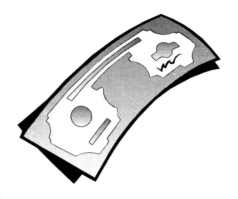

Income:

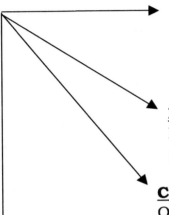

Checking Account #1 for:
Fixed Expenses

(expenses paid each month)

Interest Bearing Account for:
Long Term Savings

(vehicles, home purchase, education, church service, marriage)

Checking Account #2 for:
Occasional Expenses

(expenses which happen less frequently than monthly but on a
regular basis throughout year)

Checking Account #3 for:
Variable Expenses

(expenses which will happen who knows when, but are sure to come)

Savings tidbits:

Always save something each month, even ten dollars. It is the habit that
is important.

It is better to save more than less. There is nothing worse than a financial
surprise.

When a new savings goal is set, it is good to open a separate account.

When a savings goal is met, have a small, private celebration.

Once savings goals have been established, spend what you don't save and
enjoy it.

PRACTICE BUDGET for the month of: _____

Worksheet #36

Fixed Expenses (items paid each month)	Proposed Budget	Actual Expenses	Plus or Minus
Car payment	$_____	$_____	$_____
Car payment	$_____	$_____	$_____
Credit card payment	$_____	$_____	$_____
Credit card payment	$_____	$_____	$_____
Church/charity contributions	$_____	$_____	$_____
Dental Insurance	$_____	$_____	$_____
House payment/rent	$_____	$_____	$_____
Medical insurance	$_____	$_____	$_____
Other loan payment(s)	$_____	$_____	$_____
Other loan payment(s)	$_____	$_____	$_____

* * * * * * * * * * * * * *

Long-term savings (church service, education, home purchase, marriage, vehicles) (Plan to put away 10% of net income each month)

(to savings account)	$_____	$_____	$_____

Occasional expenses (less frequently than monthly, but on a regular basis throughout year) (Use **Worksheet #32, Budget - Occasional Expenses**, to calculate amount to put away each month) (to #2 acct.) $_____ $_____ $_____

Variable expenses (who knows when, but it is sure to happen) (Use **Worksheet #34, Budget - Variable Expenses**, to calculate amount to put away each month)

(to #3 chkg. account)	$_____	$_____	$_____

* * * * * * * * * * * * * *

Allowance	$_____	$_____	$_____
Child care	$_____	$_____	$_____
Clothing	$_____	$_____	$_____
Diapers	$_____	$_____	$_____
Electricity	$_____	$_____	$_____

PRACTICE BUDGET for the month of: _____ (continued)

Fixed Expenses (continued) (items paid each month)	Proposed Budget	Actual Expenses	Plus or Minus
Food - week 1	$_____	$_____	$_____
- week 2	$_____	$_____	$_____
- week 3	$_____	$_____	$_____
- week 4	$_____	$_____	$_____
- dinner out	$_____	$_____	$_____
Garbage	$_____	$_____	$_____
Gasoline	$_____	$_____	$_____
Haircuts	$_____	$_____	$_____
Natural gas	$_____	$_____	$_____
Newspaper	$_____	$_____	$_____
Phone	$_____	$_____	$_____
Pocket money	$_____	$_____	$_____
Recreation	$_____	$_____	$_____
Sewer	$_____	$_____	$_____
Shoes	$_____	$_____	$_____
Variety (non-food items)	$_____	$_____	$_____
Water	$_____	$_____	$_____
Other	$_____	$_____	$_____
Other	$_____	$_____	$_____
Other	$_____	$_____	$_____
Other	$_____	$_____	$_____
Total	$_____	$_____	$_____

MASTER BUDGET CATEGORIES   Worksheet #38

Fixed Expenses
(items paid each month)

Allowance

Car payment

Child care

Clothing
Dental insurance

Diapers

Electricity

Food (weekly)

Garbage
Gasoline
Haircuts

House payment

Long-term savings
(church service, education,
home, marriage, vehicles)

Medical insurance
Natural gas
Newspaper

Occasional Expenses
(less frequently than
monthly, but on a regular
basis throughout year)

Car insurance

Car registration

Christmas

Dentist

Food storage (staples)

Holidays (birthdays,
anniversaries, celebrations)

Home insurance

Home storage (non-food items)

Internet service
Life insurance

Magazines

Variable Expenses
(who knows when,
but it is sure to happen)

Birthdays (gifts, parties)

Car maintenance
Car repair

Checks

Dry cleaning

Film (processing, prints)

Home maintenance
(light bulbs, filters)

Home repair (replace roof,
carpeting, paint)

Office (gifts, meals out)

MASTER BUDGET CATEGORIES (continued)

Fixed Expenses

Phone
Pocket money

Recreation (cash)

Sewer
Shoes

Variety (non-food
items purchased weekly)

Water

Other:

_____
_____
_____

Occasional Expenses

Professional dues
Property taxes

Smog/safety inspection

Summer recreation (movie
rental, ice cream, treats)

Vacation

_____
_____
_____

Variable Expenses

Orthodontist

Prescriptions

Repair-short term sav-
ings (i.e., faucets, hoses,
bike tubes, etc.)

Repair-long term sav-
ings (i.e., appliances, lawn-
mower, tools)

School (fees, parties,
pictures, yearbooks)

Scouts (registration,
uniforms, activities)

Sports (fees, uniform,
transportation)

Stamps (postage, post-
cards, stationery)

Tires

Yard (fertilizer, seeds,
plants, supplies, tools)

_____
_____
_____

DEBT ELIMINATION - Example and Practice Sheet   Worksheet #40

	Debt 1= $200	Debt 2= $700	Debt 3= $1500	Debt 4= $2,600	Debt 5= $4,000	Debt 6= $5,700	Total Monthly Payments
Monthly Payment	100	200	300	400	500	600	2100
Month							
1	100	200	300	400	500	600	2100
2	100	200	300	400	500	600	2100
3	→	100+200	300	400	500	600	2100
4	PAID	→	300+300	400	500	600	2100
5		PAID	→	600+400	500	600	2100
6			PAID	→	1000+500	600	2100
7	CASH			PAID	→	1500+600	2100
8					PAID	→	2100
9						PAID	
10							TO SAVINGS ↓

	Debt 1=	Debt 2=	Debt 3=	Debt 4=	Debt 5=	Debt 6=	Total Monthly Payments =
Monthly Payment @							
Month							
1							
2							
3							
4							
5							
6							
7							
8							
9							
10							
11							
12							
13							
14							
15							
16							
17							
18							

DEBT ELIMINATION - Form

Worksheet #41

	Debt 1=	Debt 2=	Debt 3=	Debt 4=	Debt 5=	Debt 6=	Total Monthly Payments =
Monthly Payment @							
Month							
1							
2							
3							
4							
5							
6							
7							
8							
9							
10							
11							
12							
13							
14							
15							
16							
17							
18							
19							
20							
21							
22							
23							
24							
25							
26							
27							
28							
29							
30							

CASH

HOUSE OF ORDER - FINANCES
© Marie Calder Ricks/House of Order

Chapter Fourteen

HOME STORAGE

"Why go to the drug store every week when
you can get by with one trip a year?"
Marie Ricks

SUPPLIES NEEDED: Five copies of **Worksheet #43, "Home and Food Storage Inventory"**

Five copies of **Worksheet #44, "Cherry Picking"**

All non-food receipts you may have on hand

3" x 5" card box called the "Best Price" Box (the same box as is used for the Food Storage "Best Price" Box)

An alphabetical set of 3" x 5" card dividers (a different color than the Food Storage "Best Price" card dividers)

100 3" x 5" lined cards

GOALS: Take an inventory of staples on hand, review receipts, and fill out several "Home/Food Storage Inventory" sheets (see **Worksheet #42** for possible items to store and **Worksheet #43** for a **"Home and Food Storage Inventory"**)

Indicate :

- List items to purchase

- Size to buy

- Number of items needed

- Number of items on hand

INVENTORY

- Number of items to buy (which is the "Number of items needed" minus the "Number of items on hand")

- Proposed cost each

- Proposed cost total

Visit three favorite stores to make a "Best Price" survey without making any purchases (see **Worksheet #44, "Cherry Picking"**)

Return to these three stores again to purchases items at best price

Mark items with date stamp to aid in rotation and then store them

Complete the rest of your **"Home/Food Storage Inventory"** sheets (see **Worksheet #43**) indicating:

- Amount purchased

- Actual price per item

- Actual total price

Using your non-food receipts, prepare a "Best Price" Box with one cross-lined 3" x 5" card for each non-food item regularly purchased indicating:

- Item

- Brand name

- Size

- Cost per size

- Store where purchased

- Date of purchase

(See **Worksheet #45** for instructions on making the **"Best Price" Box**, and **Worksheet #46, "Best Price" Items List** for common items for which to track prices.)

File cards alphabetically behind appropriate card dividers

Fill out "Best Price" cards with suitable information to use as future reference

File receipts in back of "Best Price" Box as backup for future reference

Michelle had seen enough of variety stores to last for a lifetime. (We didn't even begin the topic of grocery shopping. We decided to save that for another day.) Every time she went it was always the same. Two kids to get in the car and take with her, a cart to snag, long aisles to be transversed as she tried to make decently prudent decisions about what to buy now or what had to wait for a sale. It just didn't work. She was buying a single shampoo bottle on this aisle, a box of band aids down that one. Where was the toilet tissue now and why couldn't she find the brand she liked so well? What had happened to the dish soap she was used to? And why had they moved the makeup around? It took so long just to find a few things and then it seemed she always waited in the checkout line until the kids were at the "loud" bickering stage of frustration.

She wanted answers when we talked, not understanding, just answers. And so we discussed the concept of visiting the variety store just once a year. When I first mentioned it, she looked at me in disbelief. Once a year?

"Why not," I said. "Try this. Next time you buy anything in the variety store, buy two. Pretty soon you will be buying five and then ten of those items which you regularly use. You will visit the store less, you will gain lots more time, and you will have a sense of security from shopping from your cupboards instead of the store."

Michelle did believe me, I could tell, but she said good-bye rather hurriedly and was on her way. I saw her several months later, alone this time, with a shopping cart full of items, ten of this, fifteen of that, five of those, and twenty of these. "I began to follow your plan and it made so much sense that the next time my husband got a bonus I asked if I could put it away to purchase all my non-food items in bulk. He so readily agreed, I am on a roll. We built a small shelving unit behind the back door and now I walk down the hall instead of down an aisle when I run out."

Yeah! Another student well on her way...

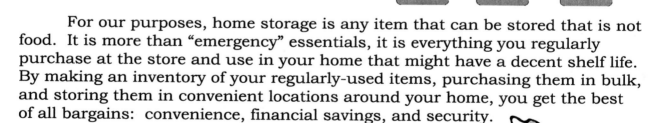

What is Home Storage?

For our purposes, home storage is any item that can be stored that is not food. It is more than "emergency" essentials, it is everything you regularly purchase at the store and use in your home that might have a decent shelf life. By making an inventory of your regularly-used items, purchasing them in bulk, and storing them in convenient locations around your home, you get the best of all bargains: convenience, financial savings, and security.

What Can I Store?

Non-food items which you purchase at a variety store can usually be safely be stored for a year, maybe two and sometimes three. So why not have a good supply of band aids, toothpaste, deodorant, toilet paper, and paper towels? If you are going to go that far, why not store an extra of everything you regularly use so that you can immediately cut your trips to the drug store in half? And if you are going to go that far, why not take an inventory, shop for your best prices, and then make one big shopping trip a year and forget about the decisions, the lines, and the time you regularly spend shopping for necessities?

How Do I Inventory My Home Storage Items?

Purchasing home storage items on an annual basis starts with taking an inventory of items you regularly use. Included in this chapter is a sample inventory sheet (See **Worksheet #43, Home and Food Storage Inventory**). Xerox several blank copies of the form and using a clipboard, walk around your house opening every cupboard and drawer. As you do so, note on the inventory sheets items for which you might want to keep a year's supply: aluminum foil, wax paper, sandwich bags, dishwasher soap, hand soap, etc. It is helpful to add brand and size to your notes at this time.

Then make a note as to how many of each item you "guess-timate" you will need for one year's time. As the years pass you will get a better idea about how much of any one item you really do use, but for now make a guess and let it go at that.

Then indicate what you think you might pay for each item. This is difficult if you haven't kept track of prices and so your best guess might have to do this first time. (A "Best Price" Box, which will be discussed shortly, might prove the answer to that dilemma during future shopping trips.)

Multiply the amount you think you will pay for each item by the number of items you want to buy to get a total price cost for each item. At the bottom of your sheet indicate (after adding up the figures in the appropriate columns), how much money you think you will need to purchase the items you desire.

How Do I Prepare a "Home Storage" Shopping List?

The **"Home and Food Storage Inventory" (Worksheet #43)** acts as a shopping list for it has all the essential information you need to go shopping. However, unless you are comfortable about the right place to go to get the best prices, you might want to consider "cherry picking" this first time around.

Where Do I Shop?

The concept of "cherry picking" is simply that you take a list of items you desire to purchase (see **Worksheet #44, "Cherry Picking"**), visit three different stores, noting as you go down the aisles the current prices, and then returning home without spending a cent. Carefully evaluate which items at which stores have the best prices. Then return to each store the next day and "cherry pick" those items which are the least expensive. Sometimes it is not quite as good as getting in on a sale, but it is a wonderfully good way to start your home storage project for the least amount of money.

After you have stocked up for the year, watching the ads and noting good prices in your "Best Price" Box will make you better informed for your next annual trip to the drug store.

The "Best Price" Box

The "Best Price" Box is a concept which will regularly save money and will make you master of your purchases. It is a project in addition to your yearly purchase of home storage and is used both for this yearly trip, food storage purchases, and for your weekly food purchases.

Basically, a 3" x 5" card is prepared for each home storage item you purchase upon which you keep track of the item, the brand, the size, the price, the store and the date of purchase. This card is filed behind the corresponding alphabetical 3" x 5" divider.

Although you have made a one-time purchase of your home storage for a whole year, you might find it beneficial and providential to keep track of the ads which might come to your home to watch for good prices, a better store with consistently lower prices, and to get a feel of the rotation of sales. Most items come on sale occasionally. By keeping track of the best prices yourself, you will have a handy reference any time you might want to make a bulk purchase. Then when you prepare your yearly inventory again, you will have a better idea of what the really "best price" for any one item is.

The "Best Price" Box goes with you whenever you shop. It is there to aid in making the decisions. Just remember to put your name, phone number and address inside the lid of your box. If you should lose it, it would be nice to get it back. Just as you prepare "Best Price" 3" x 5" cards for home storage, you can prepare them for food storage purchases. This is discussed in **Chapter #23, Food Storage**.

Why Keep a "Best Price" Box?

In putting away your home storage, you have two basic goals: 1) Getting your essentials stocked up to make life more secure and much more convenient; and, 2) To capitalize on the potential savings which may come if you take advantage of a good sale and buy in bulk.

Although it will take a few minutes to set up your "Best Price" Box and several more minutes to update the best prices you have found each time you read an ad or return from a shopping trip, knowing what good prices really are is a fundamental step to taking full advantage of "bulk" shopping on an annual basis for your home storage items.

Should I Rotate My Home Storage?

Yes, definitely rotate your Home Storage. It is easy to date stamp or write the date with a permanent marker on each item you have purchased. Some items will also have an expiration date on the label. As you rotate your home storage year to year, simply put the new purchases behind the old in your cupboards or your storage boxes and use up the front items first.

Why Should I Keep Records As To Items I Purchased and My Costs?

We not only want to make wise purchases, we also want to get the best use of our time and money. Keeping records now about what you bought, how many you bought, where you bought it, how much you paid aids immensely when you attempt to repeat the process later. It takes so little time while the receipt and the items are convenient to note on your inventory sheet what happened, and when next year comes you will be so happy you did.

Adding any pertinent information to your "Best Price" Box will make it more valuable to you when you take it shopping. You will never wonder again if you are getting a good price for you have done your homework and know the "best price".

It is really worth the effort. The professional homemaker takes her work, her time, and her finances seriously. She thinks ahead, keeps records, and makes wise choices. She does this because she has the tools, understands the principles, and is willing to make a small sacrifice in time and energy now to benefit her and her family's lifestyle for the future. Try it, you'll like it!

A prepared Best Price Box packet might make this project easier to begin. See the rear of this handbook to order or visit **www.houseoforder.com** for more details.

HOME STORAGE PURCHASES
Worksheet #42

Aluminum foil

Aspirin   - buffered
             - children's
             - regular
Baby fresh wipes
Baggies   - sandwich
             - quart
             - gallon
Chapstick
Cleanser
Clear wrap
Cold medicine   - children's
                    - adult

Cough drops
Cough syrup
Cupcake papers
Deodorant   - his
              - hers
Dishwasher soap
Dishwashing soap
Duct tape
Film
Floss
Hand lotion
Hand soap
Hydrogen peroxide
Ibuprofen
Kaopectate
Kleenex   - regular
            - small

Lawn bags
Lined paper
Liquid soap
Napkins
Nylons
Paper cups   - large
             - medium
             - small

Paper plates
Paper sacks
Paper towels
Pepto bismol

Pine sol
Plain paper
Plastic forks
Plastic gloves
Plastic knives
Plastic spoons
Pre-wash spray
Q-tips
Scotch tape
Shampoo
Shoe laces
Shoe polish
Straws
Toilet paper
Toothbrushes
Toothpaste
Tums
Tylenol
Vitamins   - adult
             - children's
             - fluoride
Wash soap
Wax paper
Ziploc bags   - sandwich
             - quart
             - gallon

Other

_____
_____
_____
_____
_____
_____
_____
_____
_____
_____
_____

HOME/FOOD STORAGE INVENTORY   Worksheet #43   Date:

Item	Size	Number Needed	Number On Hand	Number To Buy	Proposed Cost Each	Proposed Cost Total	Number Bought	Actual Cost Each	Actual Cost Total

CHERRY PICKING	Worksheet #44	Store A	Store B	Store C
Item	Size	@ Cost	@ Cost	@ Cost

"BEST PRICE" BOX Worksheet #45

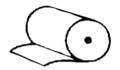

1. Collect: One 3" x 5" card box
              2 sets of A-Z, 3" x 5" card dividers (two different colors, one
                  for Home Storage and the other for Food/Food Storage)
              200 lined 3" x 5" cards

2. Line 200 3" x 5" cards into six columns, one wide and five narrow.
   Headings for each column can be added as shown in the example below.

Item	Brand	Size	Price	Store	Date
Aluminum Foil	Rey.	25'	$.50	Safe.	7/00

3. The first set of A-Z dividers is for FOOD and FOOD STORAGE items.
   These are kept in front of the second set of dividers as they are used more
   often. The second set of A-Z dividers is for NON-FOOD items (i.e. HOME
   STORAGE items).

4. Use one 3" x 5" card per item. Fill out the card when a good price is noted
   in the ads or after a good purchase. Record information in each category.
   For example: Aluminum, Reynolds, 25 sq. ft., $.50, Safeway, 07/2005

5. File the card in the proper section, behind the right 3" x 5" card divider.

6. Use the "Best Price" Box each time ads are being reviewed. Watch for
   items which meet or beat the previous best price. Use the "Best Price"
   Box each time a shopping trip is made. Compare store prices with the
   information in the "Best Price" Box. Try to beat or meet the previous
   "best price" in all purchases made.

BEST PRICE "Items" LIST Worksheet #46

Food Storage Items

Applesauce
Bean w/ bacon soup
Beans, green
Bouillon cubes
Bacon bits
Catsup
Cereal, cold
Cereal, hot
Chicken gumbo soup
Chicken noodle soup
Corn
Corn meal
Corn syrup
Crackers
Cream of chicken soup
Cream of mushroom soup
Corn chips
Dry milk, instant & non-
     instant
Flour
Gravy mix
Honey
Ice cream cones
Jam & jelly
Jello
Juices, fruit
Kool-Aid
Lasagna
Macaroni
Macaroni & cheese
Mandarin oranges
Mayonnaise
Mustard
Noodles
Oatmeal
Olives
Onion bits
Pancake syrup
Peaches
Peanut butter
Peanuts
Peas
Pears
Pickles

Pineapple
Pinto beans
Popcorn

Pork & beans
Potato chips (canned)
Powdered sugar
Pretzels
Pudding
Raisins
Relish
Rice
Salad dressing
Salad oil
Salt
Shortening
Spaghetti
Sugar
Tomato juice
Tomatoes
Tomato paste
Tomato sauce
Tomato soup
Tuna
Vanilla extract
Vinegar
Yeast

Home Storage Items

Aluminum foil
Aspirin- buffered
     - children's
     - regular
Baby fresh wipes
Baggies- sandwich
     - quart
     - gallon
Chapstick
Cleanser
Clear wrap
Cold medicine
     - children's
     - adult
Cough drops
Cough syrup
Deodorant   - his
     - hers
Dishwasher soap
Dishwashing soap

Duct tape
Film
Floss
Hand lotion
Hand soap

Hydrogen peroxide
Ibuprofen
Kaopectate
Kleenex - regular
     - small
Lawn bags
Lined paper
Liquid soap
Napkins
Nylons
Paper cups - large
     - medium
     - small
Paper plates
Paper sacks
Paper towels
Pepto bismol
Pine sol
Plain paper
Plastic forks
Plastic gloves
Plastic knives
Plastic spoons
Pre-wash spray
Q-tips
Scotch tape
Shampoo
Shoe laces
Shoe polish
Straws
Toilet paper
Toothbrushes
Toothpaste
Tums
Tylenol
Vitamins- adult
     - children's
     - fluoride
Wash soap
Wax paper
Ziploc bags
     - sandwich
     - quart
     - gallon

Chapter Fifteen

HOUSECLEANING PLAN

"Plan your work, work your plan."

SUPPLIES NEEDED:

3" x 5" card box, called the "Brain" Box

3" x 5" cards (at least 150)

Twenty-one 3" x 5" card dividers labeled:

- Daily	- Sunday	- July
- Monday	- January	- August
- Tuesday	- February	- September
- Wednesday	- March	- October
- Thursday	- April	- November
- Friday	- May	- December
- Saturday	- June	- 20_ _

Note: In **Chapter 12, "Lists"**, other 3" x 5" card projects are explained. The dividers and 3" x 5" cards from these other projects may also be kept in the back of the "Brain" Box.

GOALS:

Prepare the 3" x 5" card box and all dividers

Prepare all 3" x 5" housecleaning cards (see **Worksheets #47** and **#48, Housecleaning Cards - Daily and Weekly**, and **Worksheets #49, #50, #51, #52, "Brain" Box Cards**)

File all completed 3" x 5" housecleaning cards behind the appropriate 3" x 5" card dividers

Calendar those monthly, quarterly, semi-annually and annually housecleaning chores scheduled for the next month on your planner's calendar at the first of each month

Jane's house smelt of many things, most of them rather unpleasant. I could tell there was a full wastebasket in the house upon entering and soon saw the overflowing can near the kitchen door. There were newspapers stacked five feet high by the back door, little bits of litter all over the living room end tables and a musty smell everywhere. I knew this was going to be an interesting morning.

Jane had called the week before extremely frustrated to the extreme and wanting an appointment. She couldn't seem to get her housework started nor done. Her children were grown (which children she used as her excuse for not getting the housework done for many years) and now wondered why, with so much free time, the housework still sat undone.

Jane was an intelligent woman. She was considerably talented in music and an accomplished pianist. In fact, she did several projects for the community on a yearly basis which touched many people's lives. But her house bothered her and now she needed help.

Soon we had cleared off the coffee table enough to set up our tools: a 3" x 5" card box, some lined 3" x 5" cards, and a pen. We talked of priorities, of the number of rooms that needed to be cleaned, the frequency at which she wanted to do her wash, how often she intended to change her bedding and bathroom towels, and other such details.

We went on to examine which jobs didn't need her attention on a daily or weekly basis, but which should at tackled eventually. We talked of timing, and pacing, and diligence.

When our time together was done, she was delighted. Her very own "Brain Box" was now ready for use. Tomorrow she would begin and within a couple of weeks I promised her the house could shine and within six months every inch of it could be scrubbed and shiny. I told her to call me again whenever she felt like it.

She called about one month later.

"You just have to come over," she said. "You will be so proud of me. I have made my bed every day since we talked. I don't have any dirty dishes in my sink this morning. The laundry is already going today and my sheets are clean on the beds. Besides, I seem to have even more time for my community projects because I am not emotionally burdened with my housework and I can find things so much faster now."

It was good news to hear. Jane had won...

The "Brain" Box

The concept of the "Brain" Box means that instead of remembering regular household chores, household maintenance items, appliance cleaning, vehicle maintenance, and reoccurring projects which need addressing, you organize yourself with a housekeeping system that will be functional now as well as many years from now.

This involves the purchase or collection of a 3" x 5" card box, some 3" x 5" card dividers, and at least 150 lined 3" x 5 " cards. Prepare the dividers as stated above and the 3" x 5" cards as indicated on **Worksheets #47** and **#48 (Housecleaning Cards - Daily and Weekly)** and **Worksheets #49, #50, #51, #52 ("Brain" Box Cards)**. Now you are ready to go to work!

Good Habits and Routine

Habitual routines, day to day, saves more time and energy than most homemakers know. Interruptions are a part of every homemaker's life and they can be overwhelming because when you return to your work, you usually have to decide, again, where to take up from where you left off. With the use of the 3" x 5" housekeeping card system and the discipline to always first tackle the "Daily" cards before tackling the "Weekly" cards before tackling the "Brain" Box jobs, you will be well on your way to having a neat and clean house. It is most important to "neat" your house before you "clean" your house, and "clean" your house before you "scrub" (or deep clean) your house.

You might be is wise to set aside a certain amount of time each day for your household chores, usually a three-hour block either in the morning or afternoon. During this time you clean your house, do the wash, make phone calls, and complete your paperwork consistently and with dedication. Distraction and interruptions should be kept to a minimum while you are focusing on being a professional homemaker. This means leaving the phone to the answering machine (except in emergencies), turning off the TV (unless it is in important entertainer for young children), and working hard and fast.

Daily Jobs

The 3" x 5" housekeeping cards facilitate this goal. First thing in the morning, the "Daily" cards are spread out on the counter. Between getting the baby up and fed, your husband ready and off to work, the kids dressed and off to school, you begin working on the "Daily" cards, turning each of them over in turn when the job is done. You don't focus on any other projects or challenges because you know the jobs listed on these cards are the first priority.

Weekly Jobs

With these jobs done, you can go to the next stack, jobs which need to be done on this day of the week, i.e. the cards behind the "Tuesday" divider. These are called the "Weekly" jobs. These jobs usually are a bit deeper, take more time and commitment, and definitely need your focus.

"Scrub" Jobs

When the "Weekly" jobs are done, try to finish off your "Brain" Box job(s), those jobs which have been transferred from your "Brain" Box to your planner as needing attention today. Do this before diverting to recreation, leaving the house, or stopping housework all together.

The "20- -" Divider

The "20__" card divider is for preparing and saving 3" x 5" cards to remember items which will need your attention in future years and are reoccurring. For instance, you may decide to get a termite inspection every five years. Make up a card listing the termite company's last inspection date and the due day for the next one and put it behind this divider. Other infrequent maintenance jobs can also be tracked in this way. When the new year begins, review these cards to see which items should be placed in this year's planner for further attention.

Other "Brain" Box Projects

There are other 3" x 5" card projects which have been discussed in an earlier chapter (see **Chapter 12, "Lists"**). Those dividers and their attached cards go in the back of the "Brain" Box. They are discussed separately because they are of a lower priority and of a different purpose then the housecleaning cards in general.

If you want to get going on your housecleaning right away, the prepared Housecleaning Plan packet might help. See the rear of this handbook to order or visit **www.houseoforder.com** for more details.

HOUSECLEANING CARDS – Daily & Weekly   Worksheet #47

1. Collect: 50 lined 3" x 5" cards
                  One 3" x 5" card box, the "Brain" Box
                  Eight blank 3" x 5" card dividers labeled: Daily, Monday,
                  Tuesday, Wednesday, Thursday, Friday, Saturday, Sunday

2. When each card is prepared, the job is written in the upper left-hand
    corner.   The timing (how often the job is done) is written in the upper
    right-hand corner. Any special instructions are included on the card.

3. Prepare a separate 3" x 5" card for each job listed below:

Make beds	Daily
Start daily wash	Daily
Empty dishwasher	Daily
Fix breakfast	Daily
Clean up from breakfast	Daily
Tidy front room	Daily
Tidy bedrooms	Daily
Tidy bathrooms	Daily
Empty trash	Daily
Wash Sunday's clothes	Monday
Pay bills/tackle paperwork	Monday
Balance weekly budget	Monday
Vacuum/sweep	Monday
Wash bath and kitchen towels	Tuesday
Clean bathroom(s)	Tuesday
Clean kitchen	Wednesday
Plan weekly menus	Wednesday
Prepare grocery list	Wednesday
Vacuum/sweep	Wednesday
Wash master bedroom sheets	Thursday
Grocery shop	Thursday
Do banking	Thursday
Run errands	Thursday
Wash children's bedroom sheets	Friday
Dust/do mending	Friday
Vacuum/sweep	Friday

Wash pajamas	Saturday
Wash car(s)	Saturday
Mow lawns	Saturday
Sweep walks	Saturday
Clean children's bedrooms	Saturday
Prepare meal in crock-pot	Sunday
Gather church materials	Sunday
Write letters	Sunday

```
Make Beds              Daily



        3x5 Card
          (EXAMPLE)
```

4.   The 3" x 5" cards are filed behind the appropriate 3" x 5" card divider.

5.   At the beginning of each day, the "Daily" cards are pulled and spread out on the counter. As each job is done, the card is turned over. When all jobs are done, the cards are returned to the 3" x 5" card box behind the "Daily" card divider. If a job is not completed and it is important that it not be missed, the card is placed on its side (like a bookmark) in the 3" x 5" card box as a reminder of its priority the following day.

6.   On Monday, the "Daily" cards are completed first. Then the "Monday" cards are spread out on the counter. As each job is done the card is turned over. When all jobs are done, these cards are returned to the 3" x 5" card box behind the "Monday" card divider. Again, if a job is not completed and it is important that it not be missed, the card is placed on its side (like a bookmark) in the 3" x 5" card box as a reminder of its priority the following day.

7.   As each weekday begins, the "Daily" cards are always completed first. Then the "Weekly" jobs for that specific day are completed.

8.   Many times, the days get tough. Even then, the "Daily" cards are brought out first and as much as is possible is completed. Then, and only then, are the specific day's jobs tackled and completed. If there is time and energy, any undone cards from the previous day are completed. The undone cards are done on a priority basis. When the job is done, its card is turned back down to its proper position and put in its proper place. Sometimes, the jobs just have wait until next time. If a job is left undone one day (for "Daily" cards) or one week (for a "Weekly" card), it should be done as priority item the following time so as to keep the house systematically cleaned and maintained. Now, "plan your work and work your plan". Success is sure to follow!!!

"BRAIN" BOX CARDS   Worksheet #49

1.   Collect: 100 lined 3" x 5" cards

One 3" x 5" card box, the "Brain" Box (the same box as used
        for the "Daily" and "Weekly" Housecleaning cards)

Thirteen blank 3" x 5" card dividers labeled:

January	July	20_ _
February	August	
March	September	
April	October	
May	November	
Jun	December	

2.   When each card is prepared, the job is written in the upper left-hand
corner.   The timing (how often the job is done) is written in the upper
right-hand corner. Any special instructions are included on the card.

3.   There are five different kinds of cards: Annual "to do" projects, annual
"scrub" jobs, semi-annual "scrub" jobs, quarterly "scrub" jobs, and
monthly "scrub" jobs. Prepare a separate 3" x 5" card for each job listed
below:

Annual "to do" projects

January -	Prepare yearly calendar Organize birthday cards Organize special occasion cards
February -	Inventory home storage Make home storage purchases
March -	Review menus, recipe cards, and cookbooks Revise Master Menu
April -	Inventory food storage Make food storage purchases
May -	Update Family "Information" Binder – <u>Family</u> Section Plan summer jobs for children Plan summer activities for children
June -	Update Family "Information" Binder - <u>Medical</u> Section

"BRAIN" BOX CARDS (continued)

July -
- Update family history information
- Make school supplies purchases
- Purchase/sew/mend school clothes

August -
- Update fire insurance information

September -
- Review personal goals for upcoming nine months

October -
- Inventory food storage
- Make food storage purchases
- Plan Christmas presents, activities

November -
- Prepare Christmas cards
- Purchase Christmas gifts
- Cook and freeze Christmas treats

December -
- Calendar Christmas season traditions
- Wrap Christmas presents
- Set family goals for next year

Annual "scrub" jobs

January -   Check fire extinguisher
February - Vacuum smoke detector(s)
March -   Vacuum drapes/blinds/slates
April -   Clean out bedroom closets
May -   Clean freezer
June -   Oil sewing machine
July -   Turn mattresses
August -   Vacuum lampshades
September - Wash blankets
October -   Wash mattress pads
November - Wash bedspreads
December - Buy stamps

Semi-annual "scrub" jobs

Jan/July -
- Clean kitchen cupboards
- Scrub kitchen floor
- Clean kitchen and laundry appliances
- Clean kitchen drawers
- Scrub kitchen counters
- Clean wastebaskets

"BRAIN" BOX CARDS (continued) Worksheet #51

Feb/Aug -
Vacuum furniture
Move furniture and vacuum
Clean out hall closets
Clean wall fixtures and plugs
Polish wooden furniture
Clean and oil bikes

Mar/Sept -
Vacuum intake vents
Scrub entry and laundry floors
Wash bedroom windows
Clean laundry cupboards
Clean out bedroom drawers
Vacuum bedroom closet floors

Apr/Oct -
Wash rugs
Clean window sills/crevices
Clean light fixtures/lamp bulbs
Wash front room/kitchen windows
Clean vacuum

May/Nov -
Caulk shower/tub/toilet
Clean shower/bath walls
Clean bath drains/faucets/towel racks
Scrub bath floors
Take family portrait

June/Dec -
Vacuum baseboards
Clean venetian blinds/wooden slats
Decobweb corners and ceilings
Dust shutters/pictures frames
Dust books/shelves
Arrange for dental appointment

Quarterly "scrub" jobs

Jan/Apr/Jul/Oct -
Organize children's toys
Clean mirrors

Feb/May/Aug/Nov -
Clean shower door/curtain
Check vehicle(s) oil/tire pressure/battery

Mar/Jun/Sep/Dec -
Clean piano keys
Check and/or change furnace filters

Monthly "scrub" jobs

- - Clean vehicle(s) inside and out
- - Dust kitchen cupboard doors
- - File papers, articles and clippings
- - Write in baby book
- - Write letters/e-mails
- - Balance bank statement(s)
- - Take a day off
- - Prepare budget for next month
- - Add "scrub" jobs to next month's calendar

4. The 3" x 5" cards are filed behind the appropriate 3" x 5" card divider.

5. At the end of each month the next month's cards are pulled and the jobs added to your planner/calendar on days which seem appropriate for the time and energy needed for the job. When all jobs have been assigned a day to be done, the cards are returned to the 3" x 5" card box behind the next appropriate card divider. If a job is not completed on its assigned day, and it is important that it not be missed, the job is reassigned to another day during the month. Otherwise, and sometimes wisely, it is skipped until the next time it comes up.

6. As each weekday begins, the "Daily" cards are always completed first. Then the jobs for the specific day, i.e. "Tuesday", are completed. Lastly, the "to do" projects and "scrub" jobs for that month (i.e. the "Brain" Box jobs) are completed.

7. Sometimes, these jobs just have wait until the next time. If a job is left undone one day (for "Daily" cards) or one week (for a "Weekly" card), or for longer (for "Brain" Box cards) it should be done as a priority item the next time to keep the house methodically cleaned and maintained. So again, "plan your work and work your plan". Triumph will surely come!!!

8. Remember, you are creating a haven of orderliness which can bring additional serenity and tranquility to your family. The more skills you gain with practice and patience, the more likely your home will be both orderly and clean.

Chapter Sixteen

HOUSECLEANING METHODS

"Humans need order in their lives to function at their best. The order of our days in many ways gives us our image of ourselves."
Donna Goldfein

SUPPLIES NEEDED: One completed 3" x 5" card "Brain" Box

A tote container full of essential housecleaning supplies

A good broom, dustpan and brush, and mop

A good vacuum

Two dozen "cleaning" rags (about the size of a washrag)

GOALS: Gather household cleaning supplies, tools and cleaners

Prepare homemade cleaning solutions (see **Worksheet #53, Housecleaning Solutions**)

Do your "Daily" jobs first thing in the morning during the upcoming week to gain more discipline in your life and to get your housework done in a timely manner (see **Worksheet #47** and **#48, Housecleaning Cards - Daily and Weekly**)

Next do the "Weekly" jobs which have been assigned for today (see **Worksheet #47** and **#48, Housecleaning Cards - Daily and Weekly**)

Finally, as time allows, do one major "Brain" Box job such as a monthly, quarterly, semi-annual or annual job (see **Worksheets #49, #50, #51,** and **#52, "Brain" Box Cards**)

© Marie Calder Ricks/House of Order

Mandy had a problem. There was too much house, not enough time, and plenty of children. We had already set up a housecleaning plan which seemed to be feasible for her family but although they knew what they were to do, most of the children didn't know 'how to do"... She still needed some help. She knew the bathroom needed cleaning, but how? She felt the kitchen could use a regular scrubbing, but what needed to be done to really "finish" the job? She wanted to teach her children to clean up their bedrooms right, but where should they start? It just seemed so overwhelming to her.

She came to class that night full of questions and no idea about where to begin. So with the other students, we talked of setting standards of neatness, of breaking the big jobs (like cleaning the bathroom) down into smaller, easier steps that anyone, adult or child, could understand. We discussed timing, motivation, and tools.

We talked of letting everyone help a little bit with the laundry, the dishes, and cleaning up the house twice a day. We talked of making the house neat first thing in the morning, cleaning part of the house each day, and doing a scrubbing job to maintain the well-being of house on a long-term basis. We discussed "pick it up, don't pass it up" as a customary habit which everyone could employ. We talked of husbands that could help and pre-schoolers that could do their share. Mandy was excited. She would go home and try.

She came back the next week thrilled. She had asked each of her children to help away put some of the laundry on the days when she did the wash. She had each of them do one small part to clean up after dinner. She showed them how to do the "big five": pick up their toys and books, open their curtains, make their beds, shut the drawers, and close their closets (before they left for school). She had worked with four of her children, one child per day, teaching them simple cleaning chores in the bathroom and was astounded how well they responded when asked to help. She even got her husband to put his dirty clothes in the dirty clothes basket. It was working, and she could tell it was going to get better and better with consistent effort.

The Professional Homemaker's Way

If you are going to be professional about your housecleaning, you will need to set some parameters on your time and priorities in order to get the work done on time, without too much interruption, and in such a way as to bring satisfaction.

Every homemaker's life will be a little chaotic. After all, we are sometimes raising children, taking care of spouses, and attending to other responsibilities even as we desire to keep our homes neat and clean. So how do we protect ourselves from the inevitable interruptions which seem to undo our best-laid plans?

Three things might help: Set aside three hours per day to focus on your household responsibilities. As much as possible do not take phone calls, entertain visitors, or allow television to interrupt your focus and concentration. Some days your household chores will keep you knee-deep in cleaning solutions, wash, and vacuuming. Other days you will be out and about running errands, grocery shopping and picking up the dry cleaning. But always, always keep that three-hour block protected to focus on the essentials.

This is one of the ways those women who seem so organized with houses orderly and neat really keep that way. They work on it, day in and day out, at a regularly-scheduled time. It is their time to be a professional homemaker. When friends call and want to meet at the mall to shop, they decline until after their three-hour commitment is up. When it is time to make a doctor's appointment, they schedule it after their housework will be done. When someone wants to come and visit, they suggest coming later in the morning after the three-hour block will be over.

Sometimes, it is a matter of being in charge of your life. Declining, delaying, or suggesting alternatives usually works with the most stubborn of friends and family. "I'm sorry but I can't visit now, but I'll call you after 10 a.m." soon establishes with friends you are really serious about getting your work done first and visiting afterwards. Not answering your phone soon tells people you are not usually available until later in the morning. Asking for a specific time for a doctor's appointment usually makes your schedule work smoother, too.

So, set your three-hour time limit, keep it safe, and then go to work. Usually it is best to do your "daily" jobs first. Most of these jobs are "neating" jobs. In other words they give the illusion of a clean house because they pick up, neat up, and straighten the bedrooms, kitchen, and living areas.

When these jobs are done, then it is time to focus on your "weekly" jobs, those which are assigned to be done today. These jobs are usually more "cleaning" in orientation and keep the dust down, the floors clean, and the bathrooms sanitized.

Doing one big "monthly, quarterly, semi-annual, or annual" "Brain" Box job each day keeps the house in a continual state of being maintained, "scrubbed", and optimally cleaned.

So go to, get started. First "neat", then "clean", and finally "scrub". If for some reason the jobs don't all get done, don't worry, tomorrow will bring another three-house time block to try again.

The Magic of a Cleaning Tote Container

Some jobs, like cleaning the kitchen and bathroom, are jobs which require focus, several different kinds of tools and cleaning solutions, and usually a good pair of gloves. The tote container might have a stack of cleaning cloths, cleanser, a toilet brush, a scrubbing pad, old toothbrushes for cleaning in nooks and crannies, and a sponge. Keeping all these tools together makes for an easier cleaning session. Just grab the tote container, go to the room requiring attention and go to work. As with all responsibilities, convenience is one answer to making the job go faster and easier.

Light, Medium and Heavy-Duty Cleaning Solutions

Preparing and putting in your tote container three strengths of cleaning solutions prepares you for tackling different kinds of difficult cleaning jobs easily. The light-duty cleaner is a cleaning solution which is adaptable to all kinds of different cleaning needs: spots on the carpet, stainless steel appliances, and fingerprints on the wall.

The medium-duty cleaner is also a good sanitizer and helps in the bathroom, in the toilet, and for deeper dirt. Use it when the light-duty cleaner is not enough.

The heavy-duty cleaner is great when you want to wash down a whole wall, deep-clean the kitchen floor, or scrub off your counter tops. It is easy to make up and doesn't require rinsing.

Why Wear an Apron?

Wearing a cobbler's apron with two large pockets when doing your housework is like carrying around a wastebasket and a "save-this-for-later" bucket at the same time as you are keeping your own clothes clean. Choose one pocket for a "wastebasket" and the other as a "save" pocket. When you begin your day and walk around the different rooms picking up, stick the doll clothes in the "save" pocket, put the used tissue in the "discard" pocket, the gum wrapper in the "discard" pocket, and the marbles in the "save" pocket. When your housework is done, empty your pockets and hang the apron up for tomorrow's use.

Teaching Your Family to "Pick It Up, Don't Pass It Up"

One of the most effective tools to keep the house looking nice is to help your family put things away themselves. Closing a closet door when they walk down the hall, picking up a toy and putting it away when they see it on the floor, and pushing in their chair in after dinner are all small tasks which make a tremendous difference in the appearance of the home.

Have you ever felt like saying, "This house is such a mess." When your house gets that way, have a "Pick It Up, Don't Pass It Up" session. Everyone in the home is given five minutes to see how many items they can put away, straighten, or pick up and discard. The person with the most "pick-ups" is given a treat. After several times of this game, you will find your family will become more conscious of putting things away without "passing them up".

Should Everyone Help?

Yes, absolutely! Everyone should help. If they live in the house, they should help in the house. Otherwise they are just a guest and after some time a guest feel useless and burdensome. There is nothing like making a contribution to help each family member feel he or she is an important part of the family. So let the children and your spouse help, ask them for their support, and make it fun to participate. Compliment anyone generously who volunteers to help, who picks up, who does their jobs quickly, or who even just makes some progress. Then they will want to do it again and again and again.

So Why Try to Keep a Clean House?

There is nothing like coming home to a neat and clean house. Whether it is yourself, your children or your spouse who enters the door, peace reigns when the house is orderly, something smells good in the kitchen, and there is a feeling of control in the home. It is always easier to keep a house clean regularly than to occasionally try to bring it to that state. Your life will be happier, your children will be more content, and your spouse will love you for every moment you spend making your home a haven of orderliness and peace.

Sometimes it helps to have a sturdy set of written standards to remind family members what needs to be done whether you want the job done "fast" or would prefer a "deep" clean. You might like the prepared, laminated standards on my Cleaning Cards. See the last page of this House of Order Handbook to order or visit **www.houseoforder.com** for more details.

HOUSECLEANING SOLUTIONS Worksheet #53

1. <u>Light-duty Cleaner</u> (like "window cleaner")

¼ t liquid soap (to help make it sudsy)
2 t ammonia (non-detergent)
½ c isopropyl (rubbing) alcohol
1-1/2 c water
1 drop green food coloring (so everyone knows it is a cleaner)

Write recipe for homemade light-duty cleaner on spray bottle with a permanent marking pen. Mix ingredients and store in spray bottle. Use for all light-duty cleaning.

2. <u>Medium-duty Cleaner</u> (for the tougher jobs)

¼ c Pine Sol
2 c water
1 drop red food coloring (so everyone knows it is a cleaner)

Write recipe for medium-duty cleaner on spray bottle with a permanent marking pen. Mix ingredients and store in spray bottle. Use for all medium-duty cleaning.

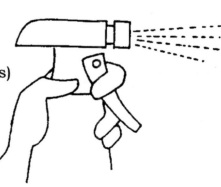

3. <u>Heavy-duty Cleaner</u> (mostly for "scrub" jobs)

1 c ammonia (non-detergent)
½ c white vinegar
¼ c baking soda
1 gallon boiling water

Mix well in large bucket and let cool a bit before using. Can be used on everything: kitchen appliances, furniture, floors, carpet, paint and varnish, etc. Items do not need to be rinsed unless the cleaner is used on windows.

Chapter Seventeen

TRAINING CHILDREN TO WORK

"As parents, our job is to work ourselves out of a job by helping our children become productive, happy, and responsible adults."
Marie C. Ricks

SUPPLIES NEEDED: 25 or more 3" x 5" cards, one for each job a child is to do during the week (the number of cards needed depends upon the age of the child and the number of children in the home)

"Incentive" job chart for each pre-schooler

"Motivational" treats for anyone that works around the house

GOALS: Begin training children to become accountable and independent by:

Helping children prepare 3" x 5" job cards for their personal use

Setting up job "incentive" charts for pre-schoolers

Motivating children with rewards/treats for improvements **(Worksheet #57, Training Children - Motivation)**

Implementing new ways to "Make it Easy" **(Worksheet #58, Training Children - Make it Easy)**

Olivia had two children. They were young teenagers and they didn't help around the house at all. In fact, Olivia was surprised when we discussed training children to work in class because her own mother had not expected help when Olivia was growing up and since her marriage Olivia had been doing all of the housework without the help of either her husband or her children. But things were different now. She was a single mother, working full-time, and it just didn't seem fair that she should have to continue to do it all at home, too.

When we began to discuss this need in class, Olivia was surprised that other mothers, even those with younger children at home, were trying to do it all themselves and feeling the same frustrations. It simply wasn't fair. In fact, to her it didn't seem right she should send her children out into the world to make their own way without skills to cope, to cook, and to clean.

So we talked of training children. Olivia wondered about setting her children down and explaining that things had changed, that she needed help and was willing to train them how to neat up the house, how to dust and vacuum, how to scrub and wipe down, and how to do dishes and start the laundry. She was rather overwhelmed at the end of the night. What if the children didn't understand or respond? What if they rebelled? What if?

Olivia came back the next week discouraged. The children had accepted her plans for change all right. They had even survived a training session where she had taught them how to straighten, vacuum, and dust the living room. But when it came time to learn about kitchens and bathrooms, that was too much.

One of the other students suggested that maybe she was going too fast. Maybe letting the teenagers learn one new skill at a time and have one new job a week would better suit her needs. We also talked about making up a list of all that needed to be done within the week and asking the teenagers how to best get the work done. This might help promote interest and involvement.

Sure enough, the teenagers pulled through. It was true too much was being dumped on them too fast. It was true they didn't like certain jobs. But one hated cleaning the bathroom less than the other and so took that job. And the second indicated that doing the laundry on a daily basis would work better than a Saturday marathon and so took that responsibility. The first didn't like to cook but didn't mind dishes. The second loved to vacuum but hated to dust. So Olivia found herself doing some chores but being relieved of others. Because they felt they were being treated as adults, being consulted about timing and preferences, her children began to act more responsible than Olivia could ever have imagined.

At our last class, she entered the room beaming. She had had a hard day at work and had called her children indicating she would be late coming home. When she did get there, dinner was hot on the stove, the table was set and her own job for the day (dusting) had been done by an 'anonymous' son.

"I truly believe in teaching your children to work," she exclaimed. "I never would have thought they could have made our life together so much easier with their contributions. Yes, it was a hassle at first to get them going. But they are wonderfully helpful now and I am very grateful."

Training Children

Because a basic part of parenting is to help children learn the skills necessary to function in our world today, it is important to understand how to train children to work around the house and yard, how to supervise them while they are learning, and how to follow up with enough motivation such that the child will want to return to their task the next time with interest and purpose.

TRAINING CHILDREN 2-6 YEARS OLD

Children at this young age are especially observant and learn more quickly if the parent actually does the job for them first to show them how it is done. Explaining each step of the process as you go along is also helpful. Then the job is re-explained again as it is completed by the child.

For instance, if you want to train a child how to hang up their coat, you would show the child as you tell them the steps: how to take the nape of the coat and put it next to the juncture of the hanger's hook and body; then how to take the shoulder of the coat and hook the hanger inside on one side and then the other; and, finally, how to carefully hold the coat to the hanger while you put the hanger on the closet rod.

Children usually need to complete the job five times with parental supervision before they are competent at doing it themselves. Then the child is given the opportunity to complete the job five more times with parental inspection and compliments. This would mean the parent would accompany the child each time they return to the house and work with them to properly hang up their coat. This procedure would be repeated approximately five different times. Then he or she would "inspect" after the child had done this job on his or her own another five times.

When the parent feels confident the child know how to hang up his or her coat, knows when it is to be hung up, and completes this job successfully, the child is left to do the job with only occasional supervision, a treat here and there to help with motivation, and generous and frequent praise.

It is very important to understand that teaching the child the "right" way to do a job and then rewarding them profusely with compliments and congratulations will do more to insure the job will be completed successfully in the future than just about any other method.

It takes a lot of time and energy to do a job five times with a child, to get them to do it alone five times with your inspection, approval, and praise and then to let them complete the job on an ongoing basis with your occasional supervision and praise. However, there is nothing like the feeling of "contribution" to make a child feel wanted and needed.

It is best to start out with at least one job for each year the child is old. The jobs for young children would best be daily jobs, ones they will do every day. They might include personal grooming jobs such as dressing themselves, combing their hair, brushing their teeth, washing their face, putting their shoes and clothes away when they get into their pajamas.

For instance, Tom is four and therefore will have "four" jobs to call his own. He might make his bed in the morning, comb his hair, get dressed all by himself (except for tying his shoes), and push the chairs in after breakfast. Sally is only two and therefore has "two" jobs of her own, maybe washing her face in the morning and folding her towel after her bath. As the child gains competency and interest, more jobs can be added according to their capacities. This does not mean children do not have other responsibilities, but these specific ones are called "their" jobs.

After a child has learned to groom and dress himself, "neating" jobs can be introduced. These include emptying wastebaskets, straightening books, pushing in the chairs after a meal, or folding wash.

Remember, if a child can get toys out and make a mess, he or she is agile enough to clean up after himself. Of course, initially, this will take a lot of parental involvement for any child works better when he or she has adult help. After several times of working with him, then several more times watching him work, and you can eventually tell him to complete the job and then return to see how well he or she could do it "all by himself".

Finally, as the child grows older and his or her interest increases, reading and writing "jobs" are introduced. These include writing his or her name, writing the alphabet, writing numbers, learning various colors, and learning right/left hands.

Memorizing their full name, their address, and their phone number are essential "jobs" for children before they leave the home to attend school or classes of any kind.

Because small and simple beginnings result is large and far-reaching behaviors, taking the time to teach a child the "right" way, the "regular" routine, and the feelings of reward and self-fulfillment are worth all the time and trouble it takes. Every child responds well to such attention and the feelings of well-being which come as they do their part to make a home function smoothly.

TRAINING CHILDREN 6-12 YEARS OLD

As children enter school, make more friends, and attend outside activities, their interest in mimicking mother and father around the house and doing "jobs" tends to wane. Hopefully, they have done enough jobs on a regular enough basis around the house that they will respond positively to new and bigger responsibilities as they mature.

For the most part, children of these ages are accountable for their personal grooming, it has become a part of their routine, and is no longer monitored except when necessary. Therefore, different and more difficult "neating" jobs can be introduced as the child matures. The goal is to help children become accountable for doing their jobs, initiate their completion without being reminded, and take pride in their work.

New Jobs

New jobs are best introduced during the summer months when the atmosphere is relaxed and time permits thorough teaching and follow-through on your part. Although children catch on very quickly at these ages, as you teach your children to work, you had best break down each new job into small tasks and demonstrate them step-by-step. It is helpful to write out the small parts of the job on a "reference" 3" x 5" job card. This makes the whole job more likely to be done completely and "right". These cards can be kept and used over and over again as each child learns household chores.

For instance, if you are teaching your eleven-year-old daughter how to clean a bathroom, she would need to understand how to shine the mirrors, wipe down the counter and top of the toilet, clean out the sink, scrub out the tub, sweep and wipe up the floor, and clean the toilet. These are the smaller steps to completing the big job.

The bathroom 3" x5" job "reference" card might read:

Clean the bathroom:
-Pick up all the trash, towels, dirty clothes, and the rug
-Straighten the towels on the racks
-Shake the rug <u>outside</u>
-Shine the mirror with a damp rag
-Wipe down the counter and top of the toilet with a damp rag
-Clean out the sink with cleanser and rinse
-Scrub out the tub with cleanser and rinse
-Sweep the floor
-Wipe up the floor with a damp rag
-Scrub out the toilet
-Return the rug to the floor
-Make sure the bathroom "shines" from your effort

After the child has watched you clean the bathroom, has done it himself with your supervision three times, and has finished cleaning the bathroom three times alone with parental inspection, "post" training and compliments, he or she can become independent. Continued parental compliments and an occasional treat makes the job easier to tackle and complete.

Regular Jobs

During these ages, there is still at least one "official" job for each year the child is old, especially during the months of school. Some jobs appropriate for this age group during the school months include such jobs as emptying the dishwasher and putting the dishes away, cleaning the mirror and basin in the bathroom each morning, cleaning up toys before dinner, helping with the dinner dishes.

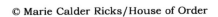

Their bedroom is also a good place to help the child become responsible for their own miniature "home". Such morning jobs as making their bed, opening the bedroom curtains, cleaning up toys and clothes, closing drawers and closet doors make for a better beginning of the day for the whole household and also establishes habits which can be beneficial for a lifetime.

Occasional Jobs

Children of these ages are mature enough to remember to do a job that only happens occasionally. Some "weekly" jobs to consider are putting garbage cans out on the curb on Thursday evening, washing the car on Saturdays, putting the wash away on Monday, Wednesday and Friday, and changing their bed linens on Fridays. Other jobs which are done on an "as needed" basis might also be added such as raking leaves in the fall, weeding the shrubs in the spring, or cleaning the gutters after a heavy rain storm.

TRAINING YOUNG PEOPLE 12-18 YEARS OLD

Our job as a parent is to work ourselves out of a job by helping our teenagers become productive, happy, responsible adults. This is especially true during the years of 12-18 for their interest in adult-like behavior is paramount, and their need to assume more and more responsibility is essential.

If they have been trained well, teenagers of this age take care of their personal grooming and bedroom "neating" jobs of their own accord. Sometimes they do not take care of their room as you would wish, but it is important to set a grooming standard, a bedroom cleaning schedule, and go from there. In other words, there are gentle suggestions, monitoring and praise, but this part of their lives is not necessarily considered part of their jobs.

Regular Jobs

Young people should continue to have some daily and weekly jobs although they may be heavily involved in school and extra-curricular activities. This is because in real life they will have "household" responsibilities although they may be going to school or holding down a job. They should also participate occasionally in the difficult and complex jobs around the house so they will become skilled at them and keep a balance in their own lives both now and in the future. One of the harder challenges youth have when they leave the home is keeping track of what needs to be done, having the motivation to do it when they don't feel like it, and getting it done in a timely manner.

Independence Jobs

"Independence" jobs are those while require more muscle and finesse, usually are not done on a daily basis, and yet are essential to running home. Teenagers of these ages seem to aspire to this type of "grown-up" work in addition to regular, routine housework. For instance, cleaning the kitchen on a weekly basis, doing their own wash, or fixing a complete meal are well within the capacity of youth this age.

Summer Jobs

Again, summer time is the best time to introduce new and complex jobs. The older a teenager becomes, the more responsibility he or she should take for running the house, fixing the meals, cleaning up after himself and younger siblings, and taking initiative when he or she sees that something needs doing.

A teenager will barely survive learning a new job once with parental supervision. He or she will usually prefer to refer to a job "standards" card to make sure the job is done completely and properly when he or she does it alone for the first time and only call for help when he or she is ready for inspection. If he or she is successful, parental inspection continues on an occasional basis with compliments and surprise treats to keep the jobs fun and rewarding.

By the time the teenager is 18, he or she should have been introduced to all household chores (daily, weekly, occasional, and complex), learned to complete them competently, and have been exposed to vehicle maintenance, balancing a checking account, mending his or her clothes, and cooking his or her own meals. Hopefully he or she is ready to live alone successfully.

SUMMARY

Training children to work, to keep a schedule, to be responsible, and to do all of these things of their own initiative takes a lifetime of patience and love. It will not always be easy. It will always take diligence and perseverance. It will often require letting some other priority go so you can show them again, praise them again, and inspect their work again. However, there is no joy so deep as the satisfaction they know how to work, how to be responsible, and how to use their own initiative. They may not always choose these routes in their adult life, but at least you taught them how so when they are mature enough to understand and appreciate the "easier" way, they will return to and/or continue in the path you shown them how to trod.

I have prepared a Training Children to Work packet to help this project along. See the rear of this handbook to order or visit **www.houseoforder.com** for more details.

TRAINING CHILDREN   Worksheet #54

Children do not do what you <u>expect</u>, they do what you <u>inspect</u>.

<u>2-6 Years</u>

Training   - each step of process explained

           - child completes job five times with parental supervision

           - child completes job five more times alone with parental inspection and compliments

           - child becomes independent with parental compliments and occasional treats to help motivation

Jobs   - one job for each year old

         - same jobs every day

         - personal grooming jobs introduced first: dressing
                                                      combing hair
                                                        brushing teeth
                                                        washing face
                                                        putting clothes away
                                                        putting shoes away
                                                        taking bath

         - "neating" jobs introduced second: making bed
                                                          emptying wastebasket
                                                         straightening books
                                                            pushing in chairs after
                                                                            meals
                                                        folding wash

         - reading/writing jobs introduced third: writing name
                                                         writing alphabet
                                                        writing numbers
                                                      learning phone number
                                                       learning address
                                                      learning colors

If you want to teach your child how to work correctly, you must break down each new task into small parts and <u>demonstrate</u> it step by step.

<u>6-12 Years</u>

Accountability
- personal grooming has now become part of routine and is monitored (only as necessary)

- "neating" jobs are increased in frequency and complexity

- new jobs are introduced during the summer months when the atmosphere is relaxed and time permits thorough teaching and follow-through

- child completes new job three times with parental demonstration and supervision. he or she uses a reference card to make sure all parts of the job have been completed.

- child completes new job three times alone with parental inspection and compliments

- child becomes independent with parental compliments and an occasional treat to keep it fun

Jobs
- one job for each year old

- some jobs are the same for every day, usually "neating" jobs:
  - emptying dishwasher and putting dishes away
  - cleaning mirror and basin in bathroom
  - making beds, opening bedroom curtains, cleaning up toys and clothes, closing drawers and closet doors
  - cleaning desk of homework and projects

- other jobs are done weekly to stimulate interest:

  - Mon/Wed/Fri – putting clean wash away
  - Friday – changing bedding

As parents, our job is to <u>work ourselves out of a job</u> by helping our children become productive, happy, responsible adults.

<u>12-18 Years</u>

Independence

- personal grooming and "neating" jobs (for their own bedroom) have now become part of their routine and are monitored but not considered part of their jobs

- "cleaning" jobs are increased in frequency and complexity as the child matures

- "scrubbing" and "independence" jobs are introduced during the summer months

- youth continues to do jobs with parental support, compliments, and occasional surprise treats

- youth learns to do all household jobs and achieves complete independence in cooking, mending, cleaning, vehicle maintenance, and care of his or her clothing/bedding. He/she is ready to live on his or her own.

Jobs

- youth does some jobs on a daily basis, but also participates in difficult and complex projects:

  - "cleaning" complete bathroom, kitchen, living room

  - "scrubbing" the kitchen floor, washing the windows, cleaning the bath tile, etc.

  - "independently" washing, drying, folding and putting away his or her own clothes

  - washing the family vehicle, checking oil, checking air pressure and battery

  - balancing checkbook, making deposits, writing checks

  - grocery shopping and preparing family meals

Stickers on charts, colored-in graphs, or any other measuring tool which indicates to the child he or she is improving is great motivation. Associate certain jobs with certain treats. A bed made gets a big kiss, the dishes done merits reading with Mom for ten minutes, hanging up your towel after bathing is good for a bit of perfumed lotion.

Some other helpers are:

- a timer: Can the child get his or her job done by a certain time and receive a treat?

- a clock: Can he or she get the job done before it shows "1:11" and get a sticker on his or her chart (which also serves to teach them how to tell time)?

- an event: Can he or she pick up his or her toys before Daddy comes home from work and fill in another square on his or her graph?

Buy-it-Back Box

Any toy that was not put away at the end of the day is put aside and the only way it can be retrieved would be through a chore, such as feeding the dog or taking care of the baby.

Or to have children buy back their items with picking up as many toys lying around as they are years old. If you have a yard to maintain, they could be pick up rocks, fallen apples, or spent flowers.

The trick also works in reverse. When children pick up after the adults, the parents earn back their strays by pushing them on the swings, going for a walk, or reading to them.

Spice-and-Span Treat

When it is time to clean up a project, toys, or a fun game, tell the children it is "spic and span" time. After the mess is cleared properly and has been inspected, the children are allowed to choose a treat from the "Spic and Span" jar. This is especially effective when friends are present for soon the children will clean up of their own initiative just for the upcoming treat.

Reading Nickels

Summertime reading goals can include "reading nickels": so many nickels for so much time reading. This money is saved and used to buy school supplies such as paper, pens, pencils, and backpacks.

TRAINING CHILDREN – Make It Easy   Worksheet #58

Color Code

Mark underwear, socks, toothbrushes and hangers with different colors, a special one for each child, i.e. yellow for Tom, pink for Susan, blue for John. Use this same color when purchasing items of the same type but of which there is a variety of shades such as plastic drinking cups, backpacks, or combs.

Organization Party

Cleaning up the small pieces of building toys such as Legoes or blocks, marbles or the plastic odds and ends from dolls will be less burdensome if they are collected in a large clear jar kept conveniently in the kitchen cupboard.

When the jar is full, an organization party is held and the pieces are divided into muffin tins with the children helping to put them back where they belong.

Each cooperative child is offered a treat for participation!

In the Bathroom

Put a second "lower" set of towel racks below the high ones for children's use. Then they can learn how to hang up their own towel without help.

Have a spray bottle full of water for taming "sleepy hair halos".

Give each child a different-colored drinking cup which can be hung from cup hooks attached to the bathroom wall near the sink.

Provide a step stool so young children can get drinks and wash their hands independently.

A single sheet of toilet paper used for a target in the toilet can save many a messy, smelly cleanup job.

A little "soft" soap squirted in the bathtub at bath time helps to reduce bathtub rings.

A timer for teenage showering saves standing at the locked door asking them turn off the water when they go too long.

Chapter Eighteen

TRIVIA

"Life can be as simple as we care to make it."

SUPPLIES NEEDED:

Address & Phone Number File:	One "rotating" type address, email, and phone number filing system
Family Message Center:	Corkboard, pins, phone message forms, pen (with an attached cord), 3" x 5" lined cards upon which are listed important telephone numbers (prepare one of each of these tools will be needed for each phone)
Secret Shelf:	Baby shower gifts

Birthday gifts for children

Birthday gifts for teenagers

Birthday gifts for adults

Bridal shower gifts

Special occasion gifts

Wedding gifts

(See Worksheet #59, Secret Shelf)

Spares:	Money to make a phone call, an extra house key, and an extra vehicle key taped to the bottom of your purse or backpack for emergencies (as you will more easily be able to call someone, get back into your locked vehicle, or get into your home)
Trip bags:	Drawstring bag or slender suitcase (briefcase) full of children's treasures and activities to be used whenever traveling (according to the age and interests of the child)

HOUSE OF ORDER - TRIVIA

GOALS: Prepare an address and phone number file using a rotating-type holder

Prepare a "Family Message Center" and post an emergency phone list at each phone

Purchase and wrap gifts for "Secret Shelf"

Gather and secure change, vehicle key, and house key in your purse or backpack

Prepare "trip" bags for the younger children in your family

Sharon wasn't good at details. She said she went to the grocery store or the variety store every single day. There always seemed to be a last-minute gift to buy or an important item which she had run out of. One day she would run out of shampoo. The next there wouldn't be matches for the birthday cake. The third day the mustard would be gone and hot dogs were hot on the stove ready for dinner. And every trip to the store meant taking an active, unruly youngster with her in the car.

Keeping addresses and phone numbers all in the same place was impossible. She had a computer address file for email addresses, a small address book she had used since her marriage in her desk, an address list of her husband's business associates on one sheet taped inside the cupboard door, and another phone list of her own family tucked in her bureau somewhere.

Finding that important phone message which she had taken for her husband meant looking on the back of all the envelopes on her desk. She could remember writing the note on an envelope, but which envelope and where was it now?

Sharon was in trouble and she knew it. There was too much to do and no organized way to handle the "trivia" in her home. It was taking too much time just to keep things up and too much time to find what had been lost. When she first got married she thought she could keep it together, but after two years and one child, her apartment began to look like her mother's home and the last thing she wanted was to repeat the patterns with which she had grown up.

She called me one day asking for help. We talked of systems, of spares, and of solutions. And, how once she had decided how she was going to keep items organized, she could begin to collect, confine and conquer. She realized she didn't need to go to the store when she ran out of something if she began to keep an extra of everything around the house. She began to understand that labeling boxes and keeping small items together in a larger container made a great deal of difference. She began to see there were specific tools and certain techniques that helped.

Finally we talked of ways to keep her child occupied in the car. She had never thought about books and toys and treasures all tucked in a bag.

I didn't see or hear from her for some time. Then one day I got a short note in the mail. It read: "I am functioning well. I can find a phone number and an address without trouble. I have an extra of everything in my house. I even like to take my son with me on errands now. I only go once a week, too. Wow! Who would have known that such small changes would make such a lot of difference. Sharon"

Address, E-mail and Phone Number File

The principle for setting up a permanent address, email, and phone number file is to make it so completely convenient and flexible you can anticipate using for years. For the homemaker, this might mean a computer, a "rotating" type filing system, or maybe a simple 3" x 5" card box. Whatever the method, it should be convenient and flexible. There must be three elements:

- It is easy to add a name, phone number, email and street address
- It is easy to alphabetically file this information
- Information can be added or deleted without causing disruption
- It is a system that can be in place for many years to come

Sometimes a "write-it-down" system is the most convenient. This might include a 3" x 5" card box with alphabetical dividers or a "rotating" type filing system. This is convenient because you can easily get to the information, arrange it, and add/delete as you desire.

Others might prefer a PDA or computer system. The only real disadvantage to a system of this sort is that PDAs and computers can become outdated, sometimes the information is accidentally deleted (as happened to me once), and sometimes your PDA and/or computer is not on or easily accessible.

So choose the system which works best for you but try to include all the elements of a truly convenient address file system.

Family Message Center

When you answer the phone there is nothing more frustrating than not being able to take a message because you can't find a writing utensil or a piece of paper. So get some telephone message forms, add an "attached" pen, post frequently-called numbers and emergency numbers, and figure out a consistent place to put messages for others, especially once you have teenagers in the home.

The message center might contain the following elements:

- a pad of message forms (pre-printed ones are best because there is a place for name, phone number, date, time, "will call again", "call back", etc. plus a place for writing a message which tends to help the person answering the phone get all the pertinent information down),

- a pen/pencil secured with a cord to the wall near the phone,

- a list of frequently called numbers written up neatly on a 3" x 5" card and posted near the phone,

- a list of emergency numbers written up neatly on a 3" x 5" card and posted near the phone,

- a stack of "in and out" boxes, one for each member of the family near the phone, making it convenient to slip all messages into the appropriate slot (so whenever someone comes home, they can check for all their messages because there is only one place to check)

Secret Shelf

The concept of the Secret Shelf is that since it is likely you and your family will be attending baby showers, bridal showers, weddings, and birthday parties for the foreseeable future, it might be wise to systemize a bit. This means deciding what kind of gift you will purchase for each kind of event, purchasing a good supply of them, wrapping them up neatly (all except the bow), and labeling them with a post-it note. The gifts are stored on the "secret" shelf until the needed day. Then all you have to do to prepare for the event is to bring out a gift, add a bow and a card, and off you run to have some fun.

There are several kinds of events which can be planned for and a good supply of gifts prepared. Making a decision as to what you will buy for each different kind of event and then consistently planning in that direction makes for a very easy life. (See **Worksheet #59, Secret Shelf**.) It also establishes a reputation amongst your friends and family as what to expect from you for an upcoming celebration. For instance it would be nice to decide what gifts you will give for the following: baby showers, birthday parties, bridal showers, graduations, special occasions (such as when gaining a professional license, getting a new job, or promotions), and weddings.

Sometimes distance and the necessity of replying to an invitation when you have no particular interest in the party involved, might suggest using money or a gift card as a gift. It is not particularly important what you choose to give, just that you decide and then have the ease of sticking with that decision and planning in that direction. It also greatly facilitates knowing how much money to put away for these expenses month to month.

For instance, Sally and Steve did not receive a garden hose with which to wash their vehicles for their wedding. So they decided they would give a good garden hose any time they were invited to a wedding. Soon their reputation for "snake giving" was well established and as their friends, nieces and nephews, and co-workers married, they began to look forward to the "snake" box which always came from Sally and Steve.

So think it through. For what events do you expect to be giving a gift for the next several years? What would be a good gift? It is amazing how much stress will go away once you have decided and all you have to do is purchase in bulk, wrap gifts occasionally, and bring out the gift when it is needed.

Spares

Being caught without a spare key to your house or vehicle, enough money to make a phone call, or any other occasional emergency need can be easily solve with a moment's preparation. Tape enough money to the bottom of your fanny pack, purse or backpack to make a phone call at a phone booth. Tape a spare house key and a spare vehicle key in the same place. Also put a spare key in a magnetic key box and attach it to the underside of your vehicles in case you also lock your purse inside your car. Think of other times and places when you have been caught without an option and plan ways to have a "spare".

In addition, the concept of having a "spare" can include keeping an extra of everything you regularly use around the house. The next time you buy a can opener, buy two and store one in a box which you have labeled "SPARES". When you get an air filter for your lawn mower, or a battery for your watch, buy an extra and put it away. Another trip to the store, finding the item again, and purchasing are all eliminated because you had the forethought to purchase a "spare" in a timely fashion.

Trips Bags

Preparing a trip bag for your children with toys, books, drawing tools, and simple games (which are only used when traveling) can really relieve the hassle of time spent together in a car. A simple, small suitcase is a good place to begin because it provides a drawing and playing surface.

And so with some thought and some work, many details in your life can be simplified. These are but a few example of "solving the problem" forever. Well, maybe not forever, but for long enough to take a lot of stress out of every-day living.

SECRET SHELF   Worksheet #59

To set up your own "Secret Shelf", make decisions as to what you will purchase or make for the following types of gifts:

Baby showers   -   Girls   _____

                     -   Boys   _____

Birthday parties   -   children 1-5   _____

                     -   boys 6-10   _____

                     -   girls 6-10   _____

                     -   teenage boys 11-19   _____

                     -   teenage girls 11-19   _____

                     -   adult men 20+   _____

                     -   adult woman 20+   _____

Bridal showers   _____

Graduations   _____

Special Occasions   _____

                                          _____

- Purchase or make up the gifts in bulk

- Gift wrap them nicely

- Stick a post-it note to the package indicating what's inside

- Store until needed on your "Secret Shelf"

- Prepare bow and attach a greeting card in preparation for the event

Chapter Nineteen

"GREETING CARDS" BINDER

"Why do something over and over when it can be done once a year and then be done with?"
  Marie C. Ricks

SUPPLIES NEEDED: One 2"-wide 8-1/2" x 11" 3-ring binder

Twenty 8-1/2" x 11" binder folders with pockets

GOALS: Purchase supplies listed above

Label the binder spine: "GREETINGS CARDS"

Label the folders:

- January   - November

- February   - December

- March   - Anniversary

- April   - Baby Shower

- May   - Bridal Shower

- June   - Condolences

- July   - Congratulations

- August   - Graduation

- September   - Wedding

- October   - Other

Not everyone sends greetings cards, but Marilyn did. She had over fifty nieces and nephews who lived far away plus all her brothers, sisters and in-laws. It was costing her a great deal of time to shop for the cards, prepare and mail them, and to keep it up year after year but it was worth it to keep in touch.

"Surely," she said when she called me, "there has to be an easier way to do it. I go to the store once a week and spend a half hour finding the cards I want. Then on the day I need to mail them, I have to address the cards (after I have found the addresses in all of my papers), find a stamps, write notes and send them off."

So we talked of buying birthday cards in bulk for children, teenagers, and adults. We talked of purchasing Mother's and Father's Day cards several years at a time. We talked of having surplus graduation, condolences, and anniversary cards on hand. We talked of how to organize everything in a binder, and how to do everything possible to make the mailing process easier.

Marilyn saw me in the store a couple of weeks later. She was approaching this year differently, she said. This year it was going to be fun because it was going to be easy. And then she asked me for my birth date. And wouldn't you know it, a card came right on time to cheer me up. Marilyn had figured it out.

One of the many trivial matters that seem to take a whole afternoon to accomplish is the purchasing, preparing and mailing of a single greeting card. We can make this a simpler job by purchasing in bulk, doing the routine parts of the job wholesale, and having a convenient retrieval system.

In January, usually towards the last of the month, once routines have become more settled, you have the holiday decorations put away, and it is a rather dull day, purchase all the birthday cards you will need for the year. This can be done either at a local store or by mail order. Tuck the individual cards and their matching envelopes together and write the name of the individual who will receive the card on the envelope under where the stamp will be placed. Store the cards and envelopes in the appropriate monthly folders in the "GREETINGS CARDS" Binder. You will know where to store these greetings cards because you have already prepared or will soon prepare the individual birthday 3" x 5" cards for the "Birthdays/Anniversary" section of your "Brain Box". See **Lists, Chapter 12**, for more information.

Also in January purchase a good supply of bridal and baby shower, wedding, condolence, and congratulations cards. Store these cards and their envelopes in the correct folders ready for easy use or mailing when necessary.

This year, before Mother's Day, Father's Day and any other holidays when you regularly send holiday cards, purchase enough cards for all your friends and relatives for several years. In other words, buy this year's Mother's Day cards, and next year's and the next during one shopping trip. Write the year the card is to be used and name of the individual who will receive the card in pencil on the envelope under where the stamp will be placed. Store the cards and envelopes in the appropriate folders.

Before graduation dates approach, purchase enough cards for all friends and relatives for several years. Write the year the card is to be used and the name of the individual who will probably receive the card on the envelope under where the stamp will be placed. Store the cards and envelopes in the appropriate folders.

Because of the bulkiness of Christmas cards, they are best handled and stored separately, usually with the Thanksgiving decorations. This makes them easy to find just about the time when you are ready to prepare them. However, it is still wise to purchase several years' worth at one time, preferably during the after-Christmas sales.

Use your expedient address system to easily find the information you need for addressing your envelopes. This topic is discussed in more detail in **Chapter 18, Trivia**.

With all your cards purchased and organized, sending off a greeting card becomes as simple as retrieving the card, writing a personal message, addressing the envelope and mailing it off. There is still some work, but only a fraction of the time and stress as before.

Cards which are not used for some reason this year will be ready for use in the years to come. Wow! What an easy way to function, early and ahead of the game, ready for any occasion with the appropriate card to give or send off!

1. Collect: One 2"-wide 8-1/2" x 11" 3-ring binder

                  Twenty 8-1/2" x 11" binder folders with pockets

2. Label the binder spine: GREETING CARDS

    Label the folders:

January	Anniversary
February	Baby Shower
March	Bridal Shower
April	Condolences
May	Congratulations
June	Graduation
July	Wedding
August	Other
September	
October	
November	
December	

3. Purchase birthday cards in bulk at the first of the year. Write the name of the recipient in pencil in the stamp area of the envelope. Put each card and envelope in the appropriate "monthly" folder.

4. Purchase holidays cards such as Mother's Day, Father's Day, and anniversary cards in bulk five years at a time. For instance, choose Mother's Day cards for the next several years. Write the name of the recipient and the appropriate year, i.e. 2007, 2008, 2009, in pencil in the stamp area of the envelope. Put the card with the envelope in the appropriate "monthly" folder.

5. The next time you have to purchase bridal shower, baby shower, graduation, condolence, congratulations, or wedding cards, purchase an abundant amount. Place them in the appropriate folder in the rear of the "Greeting Cards" Binder.

6. When you have prepared your binder and filled it with cards, you can go to the bookshelf, pull down the binder, and finish the card for use without leaving your home. What a great way to live, much more in charge of your valuable time and energy!

Chapter Twenty

"SOURCES" BINDER

"Gather all your 'shopping' information
into one place and be able to find it easily
and quickly."
Marie C. Ricks

SUPPLIES NEEDED: One 1"-wide, 8-1/2" x 11" 3-ring binder

27 8-1/2" x 11" dividers (alphabetized)

50 copies of the **"Sources"** form (See **Worksheet #61**
for a binder-sized form. If you also desire to put some
of these forms in your planner, see **Worksheet #23** for
a planner-sized **"Sources"** form.)

GOALS: Purchase supplies listed above

Label binder spine: "SOURCES"

Use **"Sources"** form, **Worksheet #61,** whenever phone shopping to
keep consistent, reliable notes in one place about the product you
are interested in purchasing

Staple to an 8-1/2" x 11" sheet of paper any coupons or business
cards which might be useful later and put in the binder

*JoAnn was building a new house for the second time. She had done a
great deal of shopping on the phone the first time she had been through this
process and had lost that important information about sizes and prices and sub-
contractors just when she needed it most. She wanted it to be easier this time
and didn't know what she could do. When we talked about her dilemma, she
was frantic and showed me her box of loose papers, none of which had been put
in any order.*
*We talked of the options. How about a binder, a set of alphabetical
dividers, spare sheets of paper upon which to staple business cards and
receipts, and a form for keeping information she gathered on the phone in an
orderly manner? It sounded great to her. She went out that afternoon and
purchased the supplies she needed, found her paper punch, and began ordering
the information she had already collected. Then she stapled the business cards*

to sheets of paper and filed them. Soon her mess was in order and she was in charge again.

She called a week or so later. "I can't believe how much difference it makes to contact a sub-contractor, call him by name, remind him that others are also giving me a good bid, and ask him what his best price is. It works, a 'Sources' Binder really works for me."

One the of the more frustrating experiences as a homemaker is to not need a piece of information at the moment and then not be able to find it when you need it. This is especially true if you have spent some time in the "Yellow Pages" calling different companies about their products, prices, store hours, and locations and have written this information down. Or, it may be you have actually visited place after place inquiring in person about their services, products, and prices and have written down information that is neither orderly or comprehensive.

How much better to have a binder which has been set up specifically to keep this information in an organized manner in a totally versatile style! This is the reasoning behind setting up a "Sources" Binder. Let's say you get excited about saving money and begin calling around to find the best price on a major appliance. By using a "Sources" form and then filing it in your binder, the information you gather will likely be more complete (because the form suggests information to gather) and will be ready and waiting when you actually decide to make the purchase.

Sometimes you will get a coupon in the mail for a service, such as discounted car rental, which you may not need right away, but which you want to be able to find when you do. Or say a salesman comes to the door with an offer to shampoo the carpet in one room of your house for free. You don't need the carpets cleaned now, but sure would like to have them done when the weather warms up. Staple that business card or coupon to a 8-1/2" x 11" piece of paper and keep it in the "Sources" Binder.

Coupon offers for eating out, business cards from friends and salesmen, printed information about xeroxing services at the local copy store, services offered by your local car repair company can all be stored in your "Sources" Binder. No more loose papers that can't be found when they are needed.

Non-food coupons (especially those with no expiration date) are best kept in this binder, too. For instance, if you get a discount coupon for lawn fertilizer but won't need to purchase any until next Spring, the coupon is stapled to an 8-1/2" x 11" piece of paper and filed, ready to be found in an instant.

The principles are easy: have a safe, convenient place to keep the "Sources" information you have gone to some trouble to gather, the coupons which you don't need right away, and the business cards you might need to refer again. It is a lifesaver now and for the years to come!

Sources   Worksheet #61

Category: _____   Date: _____

Name: _____ | Phone: _____

Address: _____

Comments: _____

Name: _____ | Phone: _____

Address: _____

Comments: _____

Name: _____ | Phone: _____

Address: _____

Comments: _____

Name: _____ | Phone: _____

Address: _____

Comments: _____

172

Chapter Twenty-One

FILES

"Wouldn't it be nice to find any important
paper you need in thirty seconds or less?"
Marie C. Ricks

SUPPLIES NEEDED: Ten file folders labeled: - 1:1-25

- 1:26-50

- 2:1-25

- 2:26-50

- 3:1-25

- 3:26-50 .....etc.

Large desk drawer or box for storing files

3" x 5" card box for storing cards, labeled the "Find a
File" Box

Five or more 3" x 5" card dividers labeled:

- Finances   1:_ _

- House   2:_ _

- Instructions/Warranties 3:_ _

- Insurance 4:_ _.....etc.

Fifty lined 3" x 5" cards

Documents, articles, clippings, warranties,
instructions, insurance and other papers to be filed

GOALS: Set up personalized filing system (see **Alpha-Numeric Filing
System, Worksheets #62** and **#63**)

Betsy couldn't find any piece of paper twice. Well, at least that is what she told me. When we visited in her home, I began to believe her. There were stacks of paper, booklets, and magazines along the walls of her spare bedroom. The rest of the house looked pretty good, but the bedroom looked like an over-sized, but under-used filing cabinet. In fact, she had just bought two new full-sized filing cabinets but didn't understand what to do next. If she did it her way, all the papers would be inside the cabinets instead of outside of them, but still wouldn't be accessible when she needed them.

"Your job," she said, "is to tell me how to get all this paper inside those two cabinets and be able to find them in thirty seconds or less." What Betsy didn't know was that there were systems which did just that. In fact, the most useful one didn't need much more than her two new filing cabinets. I asked her if she might have a 3" x 5" card box, some dividers, and a package of 3" x 5" cards. Looking somewhat puzzled but interested, she went into another room and retrieved some cards and dividers. The box she would have to purchase.

We talked of categories, what she was mostly saving, how she thought when looking for a piece of paper, and how her husband thought when he went searching for papers of importance to him. Then we went to work.

First we took several of the 3" x 5" card dividers and labeled them according to her desires: crocheting instructions, insurance papers, gardening articles, quotes for possible speeches, and on and on. Then we tackled the first stack of papers and divided them into piles as we sorted through them, putting like papers with like. When we were done, we had fifteen different stacks of paper all topped with our labeled 3" x 5" cards.

It was time for me to go and she knew what her job was: go through the rest of the stacks of paper along the walls and divide them either into the "sorted" stacks we had already started or make new ones if another category was merited.

I returned the following week to find the papers all sorted. She was pleased because twice she had needed to find a particular piece of paper and only had one out of twenty-two stacks to go through before she could retrieve the paper she needed. I told her she had made great progress but we could even make the process easier for her.

She had purchased some gallon-sized Ziploc bags as I had instructed her, a box of file folders, and also a 3" x 5" card box which we labeled "Find a File" Box. Starting with the first stack of papers, we went to work as I explained the numeric/alphabetical filing system, its benefits, and its ease of use. When our hour together was up, she was excited and almost shooed me out the door.

"I can do this all by myself," she exclaimed happily. "You just needed to show me how. Yes, yes, I will carefully choose only the best to save and will throw out the rest. Yes, yes, I will call you if I need help. Bye, bye." It was a curt farewell, but a welcome one. She was on her way to getting her files in good order and ready for easy retrieval...

Finding a specific piece of paper, especially when there is some urgency, can be very frustrating for the homemaker. Therefore, let's set up a filing system which will help you for many years to come. The system for sorting papers into categories, giving them a number under which to be filed, and making up a 3" x5" card with which to find them easily takes a bit of time initially but is well worth the effort. Such a filing system for storing papers to be kept for a long time makes for easy retrieval and for an orderly home office.

First, you decide the initial categories of your filing system. For instance, most people have financial information (i.e., school loan papers, car loan papers, and investment papers). When a house is purchased, there are many important papers to keep. There are instructions/warranties which come with the purchase of household appliances, vehicles, woodworking tools, etc. There are home, car, and medical insurance papers.

Second, you assign a number to each category. For instance:

Finances	1:
House	2:
Instructions/Warranties	3:
Insurance	4:

As your filing needs increase, new categories can receive other numbers. For instance, your husband wants to begin filing woodworking project ideas for easy retrieval. This category could be #5. You want to keep information about different landscaping and flower garden plants. This could become category #6.

Third, you initially prepare two folders for each category, labeling each with the number of its category and numbers which will be used for the actual documents. You might use the numbers 1-25, 26-50, etc. because that is about how many documents easily fit into one folder. Therefore prepare file folders as follows:

Finances	1:1-25, 1:26-50
House	2:1-25, 2:26-50
Instructions/Warranties	3:1-25, 3:26-50
Insurance	4:1-25, 4:26-50

Fourth, prepare 3" x 5" card dividers which list the category and the category number and file these dividers alphabetically in your 3 x 5" card box:

Finances	1: _ _
House	2: _ _
Instructions/Warranties	3: _ _
Insurance	4: _ _

Fifth, take the papers which need to be filed and divide them up into stacks, one for financial information, another for house papers, a third for instructions/warranties, and a fourth for insurance papers. It is a good idea to take several papers which belong together or are odd-sized, such as the refrigerator instructions and warranties, and put them into a gallon Ziploc bag. This makes them easy to keep together and file.

Sixth, take the first stack of papers, the financial documents, and begin numbering each set:

1:1, 1:2, 1:3, 1:4, and 1:5.....

until all the financial documents have been numbered. Now each document has a category number (the number before the colon) and an individual number (the number after the colon). It is best to put this number in the upper right-hand corner where it can be easily seen.

Seventh, take a stack of 3" x 5" cards and write the name of the document on the upper left-hand corner and the appropriate matching number on the upper right-hand corner.

Eighth, file the 3" x 5" cards <u>alphabetically</u> behind the right divider in the "Find a File" Box after you have made up a card for each document.

Ninth, file the document <u>numerically</u> in the appropriate file folder.

Whenever you need a document or specific piece of paper, you go to the "Find a File" Box and look "alphabetically" behind the appropriate 3" x 5" card divider for the document's name. On this card will be the number under which the document is filed. You go to the file folder with that number, sort "numerically" through the documents until you come to the right number and pull out the document.

There are several ways to avoid future problems. For instance, you might call a document "car loan statement" whereas your husband might want to refer to it as "van loan statement". In that case, a second 3" x 5" card is made up and filed alphabetically. This way, anyone can use the file to suit himself. There is no harm in making up as many 3" x 5" cards as will furnish the users with ease of retrieval.

As an end note, after you have set up this system and are ready to begin filing, carefully evaluate whether the piece or pieces of paper you desire to file will really, really be worth the trouble to file. Ask these questions:

- If I don't keep this paper, can I easily obtain the information elsewhere such as a friend who loves to file, a library, or from a book I own?
- If I don't keep this paper, will it really matter?
- If I don't keep this paper, ... Well, why should I keep it?

Remember, after you have decided you must keep a piece of paper, have it readily available for retrieval. Use a systematic way to file it and you are set no matter the circumstances.

To Start:

1.   Collect: Ten file folders
                     One 3" x 5" card box, the "Find a File" Box
                     Ten blank 3" x 5" card dividers
                     Fifty lined 3" x 5" cards

2.   Choose topics for filing, i.e. Instructions, Gardening, Woodworking

3.   Assign a number to each topic. For example: Instructions #1,
     Gardening #2, Woodworking #3.

4.   Label each folder with topic name, topic number, a colon, and 1-25.
     For example: Instructions 1:1-25. This folder will hold the first twenty-
     five "Instructions" documents. Subsequent folders (if and when they are
     needed) will be labeled l:26-50, 1:51-75, 1:76-100, etc.

5.   Label each 3" x 5" card divider with the topic name, the topic number, a
     colon, and an underline. For example: Instructions 1:__, Gardening
     2:__, Woodworking 3:__.

When it is time to file a document:

1.   Decide which topic the document is to be filed under. For example:
     "Dishwasher Instructions" would be under "Instructions", a "Making
     Compost" article would be under "Gardening", "Wooden Children's
     Wagon" plans would be under "Woodworking".

2.   Label document with topic number, a colon, and the document number.
     The numbers go in upper right-hand corner of the first page. For
     example: "Dishwasher Instructions" would be labeled 1:1, "Making
     Compost" 2:1, and "Wooden Children's Wagon" 3:1.

3.   Put document name in upper left-hand corner of a 3" x 5" card. Put
     topic number, colon, document number in upper right-hand corner. For
     example: "Dishwasher" in upper left-hand corner of card, 1:1 goes in
     upper-right hand corner of card.

4.   Keep track of available topic numbers on the 3" x 5" card divider. For
     example write: "Next number to use is: 2, 3, 4, 5, 6, 7", etc. As each
     number is used, it is crossed off the 3" x 5" card divider.

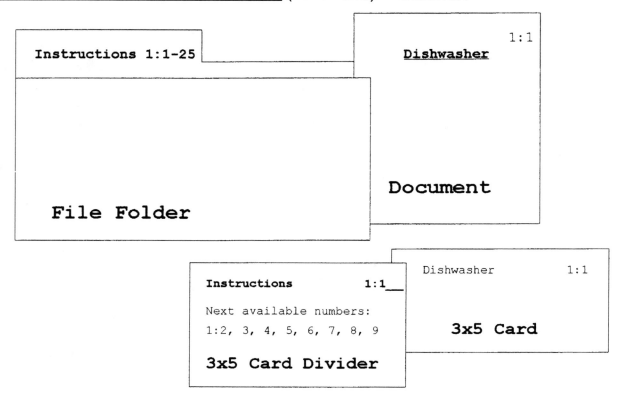

5. File the document in the appropriate place in appropriate folder. For example "Dishwasher 1:1" would be in folder labeled "Instructions 1:1-25", "Making Compost 2:1" would be in folder labeled "Gardening 2:1-25", and "Wooden Children's Wagon 3:1" would be in folder labeled "Woodworking 3:1-25".

6. File the 3 x 5" card alphabetically behind the appropriate 3" x 5" card divider. For example: "Dishwasher 1:1" behind "Instructions 1:__", "Making Compost 2:1" behind "Gardening 2:__" and "Wooden Children's Wagon 3:1" behind "Woodworking 3:__"

7. With each new document the procedure is repeated. As documents become obsolete, they are discarded. The "newly" available number is written on the 3 x 5 card divider to be used for the next document.

8. The filing system is totally flexible and infinitely expandable. It can accommodate any number of topics and any number of documents.

    Remember: the location of documents is found ALPHABETICALLY using 3" x 5" "Find a File" Box. Documents can be found NUMERICALLY in the appropriate folder.

Chapter Twenty-Two

FOOD MANAGEMENT

"Life is too short to stuff mushrooms, so make it easy, quick and convenient."

SUPPLIES NEEDED: One copy each of the **"Master Menu"** blank forms (**Worksheets #65** and **#67**)

52 copies of the "Weekly Menu" form (see **Worksheet #68**)

GOALS: Prepare personalized "Master Menu" forms to include 28 favorite main meals, seven breakfasts, and seven lunches (see **Worksheets #64** and **#66** for **Master Menu** examples)

Using your "Master Menus" and checking in the refrigerator and cupboards for foods to use up, complete a "weekly menu" for this week

Prepare a personalized "Master Grocery List" form (using the receipts of food purchases you may have on hand) and copy 52 times (see **Worksheet #69, Master Grocery List,** for an example)

Fill in one "Master Grocery List" for this week's grocery shopping circling items needed, noting quantities, calculating budget for each item, and totaling item amounts for whole grocery list to calculate potential expense

Tackle a shopping trip with a prepared grocery list, a calculator, and a commitment to keep within your set budget

Harry started out class with a whine. At first I thought he was going to tromp on his wife, but instead he made a confession. "We only have a half-eaten carton of ice cream in the freezer, some stale taco chips in the cupboard, and a bit of milk for tomorrow's cereal at my house," he mused. "I know. I ate that for dinner tonight because my wife won't get home until late. I am in charge of the grocery shopping and cooking at our home because it was one thing I felt I could handle when I retired, but I detest the mundane task and avoid it until the last minute. I don't like to make up menus, use up leftovers, or clean out the frig of moldy food. I sure hope you are going to address and solve all my problems." I assured him he would never be the same after our discussion.

"You see," I said, "there aren't too many of us that really have the time and energy to think about meals three times a day, 365 days a year, year after year without some sort of system to make it work easily and without much effort."

We went on to talk about "Master Menus", "Master Grocery Lists", bulk purchasing, getting the best prices every time, cooking for several meals at a time, storing extra food, and controlling this constant stress in life.

Harry came back the next week frustrated at me. "You should have been in my life a long time ago," he whined. "I was very careful to do as you said, and now I don't have anything to complain about to my wife. Why did you solve so many problems so fast", he continued with a twinkle in his eye. "Now I'm going to have to find something else to talk about to make life miserable".

Master Menu

The concept of the "Master Menu" is simple. Decide once and for all which main meals you will serve for a four-week period, twenty-eight main meals in all. Then use this "Master Menu" as a basis for planning a vegetable and fruit for the main meal each day of the week, one bread per day for your family if you have hearty eaters or teenagers, and one dessert to supplement meals as necessary. The "Master Menu" rotation is used over and over again month after month. The same principle can be applied for breakfasts and lunches, although usually having seven different meals, or one kind per day of the week, suits both these meals.

The process is best done by having a family council and soliciting the family's interest. What are the favorite meals of each member of the family? It is surprising to learn family members feel some frustration that "Mom" keeps serving a meal which they detest and doesn't regularly serve their favorites. When they are involved in choosing the "Master Menu" meals, they feel more a part of the decision and are more likely to support a less-favored meal when they find out their own favorites have a special place on the menu.

It is also helpful to give each day of the week a name. This facilitates the initial planning and helps to keep the specific menus in your head. For instance, Mondays are long days for most homemakers. Calling this day the "Quick" day and preparing quick meals with a minimum amount of ingredients and preparation time will help end the first work day of the week on an upbeat note.

Tuesday might be "Mexican" day, Wednesday for "Poultry" meals, "Beef" for Thursdays, and Friday as "Italian" night. It is easy to see how quickly four meals in each of these categories might be chosen by the family. Saturday lunch might be a family favorite which none never tire of such as bacon and cheese "hamburgers" with Saturday evening reserved for an "Easy" meal, maybe a cleanout of the refrigerator and prepared eggs of some type. Sunday brings "Soups" and sandwiches for lunch and "Breakfast for Dinner" in the evening.

Rotating through the meals keeps the menus fresh and interesting and yet provides relief for the cook from the eternal question, "What are we having for dinner tonight?" Soon the family will know Tuesdays are for Mexican meals and will anticipate a south of the border favorite along with corn, cornbread and mandarin oranges, for example.

Using your husband's favorite recipes occasionally makes that day special for him. He deserves it and the rest of the family can learn from it, too.

Once the "Master Menu" is prepared, long-term shopping becomes much easier. When mandarin oranges come on sale, you can purchase fifty-two cans because you know you will be needing one can each week for Tuesday night's meals. When frozen corn is reduced in price, you can stock up your freezer, should you have one, or alternatively, get two flats of canned corn for your cupboards. Each and every time you buy for the whole year, that is one less item you shop for each week at the store. Soon your meals become easier and easier to prepare, and shopping is reduced to purchasing perishable foods.

It is important when preparing meats to think four meals at a time. The same "taco" meat recipe can be used every Tuesday, once on soft tortillas, once on hard tacos, another time in enchiladas and lastly in taco salad. Thus when it is cooked, four quantities might be prepared and three put in the freezer. One preparation time and four meals are pretty much done. Then when the week begins, your frozen taco meat comes out for thawing and preparation on Tuesday.

Your "Italian" meat sauce might be prepared in the same way for Friday nights. Four quantities are prepared at the same time and three are frozen. The meat sauce is removed from the freezer on Monday and prepared along with a pasta on Fridays. One week it is noodles, one week macaroni, the third week lasagna and the fourth spaghetti.

The stress of meals is gone, a system is in place which works well, and everyone is pleased and secure. Each day of the week brings its own vegetables, fruit, bread and dessert. Everyone knows what's for dinner and general nutrition is improved.

Occasionally changes are made when a holiday ham needs using up or the mood calls for a spontaneous menu, but in general the days of the week are structured in their meal-orientation and preparation.

Updating the Master Menu

Lastly, about once a year, go through the Master Menu and make changes as necessary. Sometimes a popular meal loses face when someone leaves the home and the ones left in the home are not as partial to it. Other times everyone becomes tired of a particular recipe and it should be relegated to the back of the recipe box.

Once the twenty-eight meals are decided upon, a 3" x 5" recipe card might be prepared for each of these favorite meals. They are sorted and kept behind 3" x 5" card dividers labeled Sunday through Saturday, four recipes to each divider. Then this set of recipes is put in the front of the recipe box. This simple procedure makes the recipes immediately accessible to the cook for the night. No more looking for recipes in cookbooks, recipes gathered in drawers, or ones slipped somewhere into your recipe box.

Remember, once the "Master Menu" is in place and posted on the cupboard door, long-term purchases made to accommodate its use, and recipe cards made up for the twenty-eight meals, everything will be easier, more fun, and less stressful all around. Try it, it will make more sense and bring greater organization to your kitchen than almost any other single change you can make. A "Master Menu" is for every homemaker! My "Master Menu" Cookbook has some great "Master Menu" recipes for you. See the rear of this handbook to order it or **www.houseoforder.com** for more details.

Grocery Shopping

There are several principles to improved grocery shopping. They include always having a prepared grocery list when you enter the store, shopping when you are not hungry and with as few family members as possible, having a calculator handy to compare prices, and using your "Best Price" Box (See **Chapter #14, Home Storage**, for a detailed explanation).

The well-prepared grocery list acts like a "planner" for your trip. You know exactly which items you are shopping for, how many you want to purchase, what budget you must confine yourself to, and what aisles you will go up and down during your visit.

If you are not hungry, you tend to make wiser choices. Fewer distractions from family and friends keeps the grocery cart full of items you really need, not additions which you don't really want.

A calculator gives you an immediate response as you compare prices and sizes. Remember the smaller item may, in fact, be the cheapest. It just depends on the day of the week and the sales at hand.

The "Best Price" Box is a handy tool for the occasional question as to what is the best price for this item. You will never be caught wondering at an end cap whether this is a decent sale or just a promotion.

Saving Money Even as You Prepare Delicious Meals

There are two things to remember as you prepare menus and do your grocery shopping. You are in charge of where your dollars are spent. Sometimes it pays to back away from the scene for a minute and ask yourself where you are "investing" your money and if it might be better invested elsewhere. Could you buy foods with greater nutrition for their monetary value? Could you begin to make up some of your own mixes?   Could you reduce the amount of sweets and increase the amounts of fruits and vegetables? All these questions are important for the effective homemaker to occasionally ask. See **Worksheets #70, #71**, and **#72** for cost comparisons, assessments about regarding making versus buying, and several favorite homemade mixes to reduce the food budget.

Your "Personalized" Recipe Box

The organized homemaker understands her recipes need to be accessible and well-organized. This might mean keeping your "Master Menus" recipes in the front of the recipe box, keeping traditional, well-loved recipes next, and relegating recipes which are worth keeping but are not used frequently in the back of the box. Any over-sized recipes can be kept in a "personalized" recipe binder. See **Worksheet #73** for instructions on preparing a workable recipe box and/or recipe binder for your kitchen.

Food management takes a lot of time and energy. Every little step, every moment saved, every idea implemented means more structure to your day, more time in your life, and more satisfied family members. Good luck! Meal preparation three times a day never looked so good!

Day/Name	Main Dish	Bread	Vegetable	Fruit
Monday	Pork & Bean Casserole	Honeyed Toast	Celery	Mandarin. Oranges
Quick	Crescent Casserole			
	French Fry Burger Pie			
	Yakamish			
Tuesday	Soft Tacos	Cornbread	Corn	Peaches
Mexican	Chili & Chips			
	Enchiladas			
	Hard Tacos			
Wednesday	Oven Chicken Casserole	Biscuits	Carrots	Bananas
Poultry	Chicken Macaroni			
	Tuna Noodle			
	Luscious Lemon Chicken			
Thursday	Porcupine Meatballs	Rolls	Beans	Pears
Beef	Meatloaf/Rice			
	Primary Five-Hour Stew			
	No-Peek Casserole			
Friday	Spaghetti	Bread Sticks	Salad	Pineapple
Italian	Macaroni Beef			
	Lazy Day Lasagna			
	Mock Stroganoff			
Saturday	Sloppy Joes	Fried Pears	Peas	Apples
Easy	Hamburgers			
	Meatball Heroes			
	Chicken Gumbo Burgers			
Eggs	Fried Eggs	Toast	Celery	Orange Julius
	Cyclops	- -		
	Scrambled Eggs	Toast		
	Boiled Eggs	Toast		
Sunday	Bean w/ Bacon Soup	Melted Cheese	Cucumbers	Peaches
Soup	Chicken Noodle Soup			
	Tomato Soup			
	Vegetable Beef Soup			
Breakfast	French Toast	- -	Carrots	Applesauce
for Dinner	Hootenany	- -		
	Pancakes	- -		
	Waffles	- -		

Worksheet #64

Day/Name	Main Dish	Bread	Vegetable	Fruit
Monday				
Quick				
Tuesday				
Mexican				
Wednesday				
Poultry				
Thursday				
Beef				
Friday				
Italian				
Saturday				
Easy				
Eggs				
Sunday				
Soup				
Breakfast				
for Dinner				
Worksheet #65				

Day	Breakfast	Day	Lunch
Monday	Swedish Bread	**Monday**	Tuna Sandwiches
	Orange Juice		Carrots
	Milk		Milk
Tuesday	Cold Cereal	**Tuesday**	Peanut Butter & Jelly
	Grape Juice		Celery
	Milk		Milk
Wednesday	Swedish Bread	**Wednesday**	Egg Salad Sandwiches
	Orange Juice		Carrots
	Milk		Milk
Thursday	Cold Cereal	**Thursday**	Bologna Sandwiches
	Grape Juice		Cucumbers
	Milk		Milk
Friday	Swedish Bread	**Friday**	Roast Beef Sandwiches
	Orange Juice		Carrots
	Milk		Chocolate Milk
Saturday	Granola	**Saturday**	Sloppy Joes
	Raisins		Hamburgers
	Peanuts		Meatball Heroes
	Milk		Chicken Gumbo Burgers
Sunday	Coffee Cake	**Sunday**	Bean w/ Bacon Soup
	French Puffs		Chicken Noodle Soup
	Orange Julius Muffins		Tomato Soup
Worksheet #66	Bannack		Vegetable Beef Soup

Day	Breakfast	Day	Lunch
Monday		Monday	
Tuesday		Tuesday	
Wednesday		Wednesday	
Thursday		Thursday	
Friday		Friday	
Saturday		Saturday	
Sunday		Sunday	
Worksheet #67			

Breakfast/Lunch　　　　　　　　　**Snacks/Dinner**　Weekly Menu

S
U
N
D
A
Y
M
O
N
D
A
Y
T
U
E
S
D
A
Y
W
E
D
N
E
S
D
A
Y
T
H
U
R
S
D
A
Y
F
R
I
D
A
Y
S
A
T
U
R
D
A
Y

FRESH FRUIT
apples
bananas
grapes
oranges

FRESH VEGETABLES
asparagus
broccoli
cabbage
carrots
celery
cherry tomatoes
cucumbers
green onions
lettuce
mushrooms
onions
peppers
potatoes
squash
tomatoes

SOUPS & SAUCES
bean w/ bacon
catsup
cm. of mush.
mayonnaise
minestrone
mustard
salad dressing
soy sauce
tomato sauce
tomato
vegetable

CANNED FRUIT & JUICE
applesauce
grapefruit
lemon juice
peaches
pears
pineapple
pumpkin
raisins
prunes

STAPLES
bread
brown sugar
cold cereal
corn chips
corn meal
crackers
flour
granola
hamburger buns
hot dog buns
lasagna
macaroni-large
macaroni-small
noodles
oatmeal
popcorn
potato chips
rice
spaghetti
sugar
taco shells

CANNED VEGETABLES
beans
corn
olives
potatoes
sauerkraut

OTHER
cupcake papers
corn syrup
cheesecake
jam
jello
Kool-Aid
pancake syrup
pickles
relish
soda pop
vinegar
yeast

MEAT
chicken
fish
hamburger
hot dogs
luncheon meat
roast
steak
stew meat
tuna
turkey

DAIRY & FRIG.
cheese
dream whip
eggs
margarine
milk
powd. milk
ref. biscuits
sour cream
tortilla shells

SPICES
bacon bits
basil
bay leaves
celery salt
cinnamon
cm. of tartar
garlic
gravy mix
mustard
nutmeg
onion bits
onion soup
paprika
parsley
sage
salt
thyme
vanilla

HOUSEHOLD
aluminum foil
baggies
cleanser
clear wrap
Clorox
dish soap
dishwasher soap
hand soap
kotex
liquid soap
napkins
paper cups
paper plates
paper sacks
paper towels
pine sol
plastic silverware
pre-wash spray
toilet paper
wash soap
wax paper
ziplocs

FROZEN
hash browns
French fries
onion rings
orange juice
rolls
TV dinners
waffles

HOUSE OF ORDER - FOOD MANAGEMENT © Marie Calder Ricks/House of Order Worksheet #69

FOOD COST COMPARISONS   Worksheet #70

3 cold cereals per week $ 7.50
    ($2.50 each)   x   52 weeks
              $390.00 per year

OR:

24/16 oz. green beans	@ $.50	$ 12.00
24/16 oz. corn	@ .50	12.00
24/17 oz. green peas	@ .50	12.00
24/16 oz. peaches	@ .90	21.60
24/16 oz. pears	@ .90	21.60
24/16 oz. pineapple	@ .90	21.60
24/10 oz. chicken noodle soup	@ .40	9.60
24/10 oz. bean with bacon soup	@ .60	14.40
24/10 oz. tomato soup	@ .40	9.60
24/64 oz. apple juice	@ 1.00	24.00
24/46 oz. tomato juice	@ 1.00	24.00
5 lb. corn meal	@ 3.00	3.00
24/5 lb. flour	@ .90	21.60
10/4 lb. powdered milk	@ 6.00	60.00
12/5 lb. sugar	@ 1.80	21.60
12/48 oz. salad oil	@ 2.00	24.00
12/3 lb. shortening	@ 2.30	27.60
6/1 lb. macaroni	@ .80	4.80
6/1 lb. spaghetti	@ 1.00	6.00
5/1 lb. noodles	@ .80	4.00
50/6 oz. tuna	@ .70	35.00

402 Total Items   **$390.00** per year

Buy: Hot chocolate mix –

Carnation (brand name) 30 oz. 4 t./serving	@ $4.50	$.15/serving
Generic (brand name) 32 oz. 2 t./serving	@ 2.99	$.05/serving
Herseys (brand name) 28 oz. 2-3 t./serving	@ 3.39	$.075/serving

Fresh milk-   1 gallon   @ 2.56 $.16/cup

Hot chocolate prepared with store mix and fresh milk costs between
$.21 and **$.31** per cup

Make: Mix Ingredients-

Cocoa, 16 oz.	@ $4.00	$.13/tablespoon
Sugar, 5 lbs.	@ 1.75	$.12/cup
Powdered Milk, 20 qt.	@ 8.79	$.11/cup

Recipe-

3 T cocoa	@ $ .39
1 c sugar	@ .12
3-1/4 c powdered milk	@ .36

Makes: 4-1/2 c mix   @ $ .87

divided by 13 portions (1/3 c each)   @ $ .07/portion

Hot chocolate prepared with homemade mix costs about **$.07** per cup

MAKE-A-MIX *(equal to Bisquik)*

26-1/2 c flour
¾ c baking powder
3 T salt
2 T cream of tartar
1 T baking soda
4-2/3 c dry milk
7 c shortening (1-3 lb. can)

Mix dry ingredients in very large bowl. Add one half of the shortening, mix well with electric mixer. Add rest of shortening, mix well. Store up to six months in sealed container in cool place.

– – –

GRANOLA

1-1/2 c white sugar
1-1/3 c margarine
2/3 c peanut butter
½ t salt
2 t vanilla
1 c water

Mix above ingredients and heat in glass measuring cup in microwave for 4 minutes on "HIGH".

Mix with: 12 c rolled oats
              1 t cinnamon

Spread onto two small, greased cookie sheets. Bake at 325 degrees for 25 minutes. Exchange cookie sheets on oven racks. Bake 10 minutes. Turn oven off and let granola dry for several hours inside. Break apart and store in airtight container. Make 24 cups.

– – –

ONION SEASONING MIX

4 t instant beef bouillon granules
8 t dried, minced onion
1 t onion powder
¼ t bon appetit seasoning

Mix and store in a cool, dry place. Use within 6 months. Equal to one package onion soup mix.

– – –

HERBED BUTTERMILK DRESSING

1 c buttermilk
1 c mayonnaise
1-1/2 t parsley
½ t salt
½ t dried onion
½ t dried oregano
¼ t dried basil
¼ t dried tarragon
1/8 t dried garlic
¼ t black pepper
1-1/2 t vinegar

Combine ingredients, mix well and refrigerate. Equal to ranch-style dressing.

"RECIPE" BOX AND BINDER   Worksheet #73

1. Collect for recipe box: One 3" x 5" recipe card box
   Seven blank 3" x 5" card dividers
   Two sets of "recipe" card dividers
   50 lined 3" x 5" cards

   Collect for recipe binder: One 8-1/2" x 11" binder
   Twenty-five clear 8-1/2" x 11" sheet protectors
   Approximately fifteen 8-1/2" x 11" binder dividers

2. Label seven blank 3" x 5" card dividers: Sunday, Monday, Tuesday, Wednesday, Thursday, Friday, Saturday. The "Master Menu" recipes go behind the "Master Menu" (Sunday through Saturday) dividers in the front of the 3" x 5" "Recipe" Box.

3. The first set of "recipe" card dividers goes behind the "Master Menu" Sunday – Saturday dividers. Use this set of "recipe" card dividers for regularly-used recipes. Keep only the best and favorite recipes for this section.

4. The second set of "recipe" card dividers goes behind the first set. Use this second set of card dividers for infrequently-used recipes. Keep all viable but less-used recipes in this section.

5. Label the spine of the binder "Recipes". Prepare the binder dividers with labels identical to the recipe card dividers you have purchased. Place the dividers in the binder. Put your oversized recipes in the sheet protectors. Put these protectors behind the appropriate divider.

6. Make 3" x 5" reference cards for recipes which are located in printed cookbooks and your own "Recipes" Binder and put them in your "Recipe" Box. For example, *Bagels: See Bread Baking Book, page 33* **or** *Raspberry Slush: See "Recipe" Binder under "Drinks"*.

Clean out recipe box	Annually

Clean out recipe book	Annually

7. Update both the recipe box and your personal recipe binder annually (maybe during the month of March). Discard recipes which are no longer interesting or viable. Eliminate duplication wherever possible. It takes only one good brownie recipe to keep a family happy. Happy cooking!.

Chapter Twenty-Three

FOOD STORAGE

"Eat what you store and store what you eat."

SUPPLIES NEEDED: Five copies of **Worksheet #43, "Home and Food Storage Inventory"**

Five copies of **Worksheet #44, "Cherry Picking"**

3" x 5" card box, called the "Best Price" Box (the same box as is used for the Home Storage "Best Price" Box)

An alphabetical set of 3" x 5" card dividers

100+ lined 3" x 5" cards

GOALS: Purchase the above-listed supplies

Using food receipts you may have on hand, prepare a list of staples (non-refrigeratored/non-frozen foods) to be stored (see **Worksheet #74, Food Storage Purchases**, for examples of items to store)

Prepare several "Food and Home Storage Inventory" sheets (see **Worksheet #43, "Home and Food Storage Inventory"**) with:

- Date of inventory

- Items to be purchased

- Amount needed for six/twelve months

- Current number of items at hand

- Amount to purchase

- Proposed budget per item

- Proposed total budget

- Actual expense per item

- Actual total expense

© Marie Calder Ricks/House of Order

Take an inventory of food staples on hand, filling out inventory sheets to indicate items to be purchased, amounts to be purchased, and proposed budgets

Visit three favorite stores to make a "best prices" survey without making any purchases (use **Worksheet #44, Cherry Picking**)

Return to stores a second time to purchase foods at best price

Mark items with month/year using a date stamp to aid in rotation

Store items

Complete inventory sheets and save receipts for reference (this will make the next purchase will be easier and more effective)

Prepare a "Best Price" 3" x 5" card box with a card for each item of food purchased (see **Worksheet #45, "Best Price" Box**, for instructions on making the "Best Price" Box and **Worksheet #46, Best Price "Items" List**, for common items to track)

Indicate on each card:

- Type of food

- Brand name

- Size

- Cost per size

- Store where purchased

- Date of purchase

Jessica was a young mother. She simply didn't have the time to think about very much of anything. There were three children under five and her biggest challenge was answering all the constant questions. She felt one place she could relieve some pressure in her life was to reduce the number of times she grocery shopped and time she spent in the store. When she called, I was quick to agree. She was shopping about three times a week, almost always with her children, and she was spending far more than she really felt she could afford.

I offered to visit with her in her home the following week while her children were napping. We had a delightful conversation. Her system of grocery shopping and cooking was the most spontaneous I had ever seen. "I put the kids in the car about an hour before dinner and when I arrive at the store, I try to think of three main meals we would enjoy and then go up and down the aisles getting the food I need for those three meals, plus some luncheon meat for sandwiches and a couple of boxes of cereal."

I knew Jessica was in for a surprise as we began talking about some alternatives. We shared ideas about shopping once every six months for canned foods, boxed cereals and crackers, pasta, flour, sugar and salt. We talked of where she might store a supply of these items should the opportunity come to her to have them at her home instead of at the store. She was quick to respond she would gladly purchase some 4-gallon buckets, give up the wall of a small bedroom in order to stack food along one wall, and have her husband help her make some simple shelves in the garage for the canned goods.

We worked through Jessica's typical menus and found that more than 60% of the food she was acquiring could be purchased in bulk. We discussed purchasing two when she needed one for the next several months until her husband got his bonus and then using that spare money to make purchases which would last for six months. We talked of sources for good, sealed food storage buckets, how to label, how to rotate, and the many benefits of having a "home" grocery store.

And so Jessica began to shop a little less often. Her initial goal was to shop for a week, purchasing at least three items in doubles to begin her food storage program, and working with her husband to construct the shelving.

When his bonus came through, we went shopping together. By that time, she had her "Best Price" Box all prepared and along with my own, we were able to compare prices and make prudent purchases. She was overjoyed, really overjoyed. She figured this simple change in her routine would save her hours and hours every month. In addition, her family would have greater security and her life would be more peaceful.

She called me about seven months later. "Help," she said. "My friend wants to do it, too." "Good," I replied. "You know what she needs, you know how to do it. Call me if you get stuck..." She didn't. I didn't think she would. She was a pro now and ready to spread the good news.

What is Food Storage?

Food storage is the purchase, storage, and rotation of regularly-used non-perishable foods (those which can sit on a pantry shelf for a decent period of time) to facilitate better use of time, energy and money. Just think, once you have found a good brand, a good size, and decent price on a type of food, say peanut butter, why not buy enough to last your family for a whole year? This decision is made once a year instead of every time you need another jar of peanut butter. Think what would happen if you made an inventory of your food supplies, decided how much more you might need of non-perishable foods for a whole year and then make one big shopping trip to price foods and another to purchase them. It is more work focused in a shorter period of time, but then less work for the whole rest of the year.

It is wonderful after you have purchased your food to "shop" by going to the cupboard any time you run out of a item, instead of having to drive to the store, go in, choose the kind, brand, and size plus wonder if you are getting a good price, wait in line, go through the check stand, and return home, all the time thinking there must be a better way.

What Can I Store?

Any food that you purchase regularly and sits upon your shelf for a month or more probably has a life span of at least one year. Most foods have a date on them of "Best Purchased By" and are good for some time past that date. Packaging processes and preservatives keep the food in good shape on your shelf at home just as they have been kept in the warehouses and on the grocery store shelves.

Therefore, storing the foods you regularly eat might be a very good place to start. Usually, you don't want to buy food in bulk quantities you have not tasted yourself. But if your family likes it and it is likely you will be serving it regularly, stock up.

How Do I Go About Inventorying My Current Food Supplies?

Using the inventory sheets (see **Worksheet #43, Home and Food Storage Inventory**), go from cupboard to cupboard, listing the name, brand (if desired), size, and number of items for each kind of food.

The first time you do an inventory, you will have to "guess-timate" the number of items you will need for a year. But if you regularly use one can of green beans per week, 50 cans will probably get you through the year nicely. If you serve chicken noodle soup only once a month, twelve cans will be your purchase target.

First you indicate the items and details for the foods you have on hand. Then you add to the list any items which you might wish to have a better supply of but which are missing from your cupboards at this time. Then you decide how many you will need for a year's supply. Add the price you anticipate paying for each item, and the total anticipated cost. You are now ready to shop.

How Do I Prepare a Grocery List?

The food inventory you have just completed acts as your initial grocery list. It includes the foods you wish to buy, the price you desire to pay and number of items you wish to purchase. Transferring the necessary food items, brand, and size information to your cherry picking sheet will prepare you for the next step (See **Worksheet #44, Cherry Picking**). I will now explain what this means.

Where Do I Shop?

The first time you do your food storage shopping you will be shopping rather blindly. The most effective way to make sure you are getting the best available prices is to "cherry pick". This means you will be in charge of which purchases you make at which store. You will probably need an afternoon or evening without distractions. You will want to choose your favorite three grocery stores. These names are listed at the top of your cherry picking worksheet.

Using a clipboard for support, you go up and down the aisles of these three stores pricing the foods you are interested in. At this point you make no purchases, just price the foods.

Once you have returned home, go through your sheets and circle the price which is lowest for each item. Then compare these prices to those anticipated prices you have listed on your inventory. If you have found a store with the item at or below the price you anticipated you are set. If not, you will have to decide if you are willing to buy at the lowest price you have found or wait for a good sale. In any case, tomorrow you will be busy.

How Do I Know If I Am Getting the Best Prices?

Return to the same three stores where you did your price comparing and "cherry pick". This means, of course, purchasing those items at the first store which turned out to be lowest in price, those items at the second store which were lowest in price there, and then finishing off your project with a final trip to the third store.

How Do I Date, Store and Rotate the Food?

When you get home, you have three things to do: 1) date stamp all the food. This can be done with a permanent marker or a date stamp. It is best to date the food where the date can easily be seen. 2) Find a place to store the food. If possible, try to make all your purchases in sealed boxes for these are easiest to put away in closets and under beds. However, flats of cans can also be stacked neatly and are easier to slip into the small places. Experience has shown it is best not to worry about where you will put the food until you get home because places always seem to appear once the food is purchased. And finally, 3) complete your food inventory sheet information. This information will prove vital when you purchase food storage again next year. It will be easier the second time around and you will be more comfortable with the whole process, plus you will be more convinced having food stored at home is better than anything you may have done before.

How Do I Complete My Records So I Can Do This Easier Next Time?

It is important to write down how much food was purchased, the price that was paid, and the total purchase price for all the purchased foods. This gives you a good idea of the amount of money you will need one year from now to make a similar purchase. When you inventory next year, you will probably have a few grocery items left and will have run out of others. Make adjustments on your new inventory sheets accordingly and go for it.

What Are the Long Term Advantages of Such a Plan?

There are so many advantages to such a food storage plan it is hard to completely understand. Once you have shopped this way for a year or two, you will wonder how you ever shopped so inconsistently and confusedly before. You always seem to have on hand the food you need, you shop less often, you spend much less time in the store, you make decisions once a year instead of weekly, and your whole system of handling your food supply seems to be in control instead of at the mercy of the grocery store.

In addition, you have a new level of security. If things went sour or bad in your personal life, if your income dropped or ceased for a period of time, there would be food in your house to supplement your regularly purchased fresh foods and your family would eat well for some time to come.

Try the plan; you will love it! Remember to squirrel away food today is to feast tomorrow!

The "Best Price" Box

Now, a final note. The "Best Price" Box is a concept which will help you regularly save money and will make you master of your food purchases. It is a project in addition to your yearly purchase of food storage and is used both for this yearly trip and for your weekly food purchases.

Basically a 3" x 5" card is prepared for each food you regularly purchase upon which you keep track of the item, the brand, the size, the price, the store and the date of purchase. This card is filed behind the corresponding alphabetical 3" x 5" divider in the "Best Price" Box. The "Best Price" Box is discussed in greater detail in **Chapter #14, Home Storage**.

Most foods come on sale seasonally. For instance, baking items seem to be at their lowest prices around the winter holidays, tomato sauce and soup seem to come down at the end of the summer harvest, canned goods seem to be at their lowest at the first of the year. By keeping track of the best prices yourself, you will have a handy reference any time you make either a weekly purchase or a bulk one. Then when you prepare your yearly inventory again, you will have a better idea of what a really "best price" for any one item is.

So carry your "Best Price" Box with you whenever you shop. It will really help!

FOOD STORAGE PURCHASES   Worksheet #74

Applesauce
Bean w/ bacon soup
Beans, green
Bouillon cubes
Bacon bits
Catsup
Cereal, cold
Cereal, hot
Chicken gumbo soup
Chicken noodle soup
Corn
Corn meal
Corn syrup
Crackers
Cream of chicken soup
Cream of mushroom soup
Corn chips
Dry milk, instant & non-instant
Flour
Gravy mix
Honey
Ice cream cones
Jam & jelly
Jello
Juices, fruit
Kool-Aid
Lasagna
Macaroni
Macaroni & cheese
Mandarin oranges
Mayonnaise
Mustard
Noodles
Oatmeal
Olives
Onion bits
Pancake syrup
Peaches
Peanut butter
Peanuts
Peas
Pears
Pickles
Pineapple

Pinto beans
Popcorn
Pork & beans
Potato chips (canned)
Powdered sugar
Pretzels
Pudding
Raisins
Relish
Rice
Salad dressing
Salad oil
Salt
Shortening
Spaghetti
Sugar
Tomato juice
Tomatoes
Tomato paste
Tomato sauce
Tomato soup
Tuna
Vanilla extract
Vinegar
Yeast

Other

_____
_____
_____
_____
_____
_____
_____
_____
_____
_____
_____
_____

Item	Size	Number Needed	Number On Hand	Number To Buy	Proposed Cost Each	Proposed Cost Total		Number Bought	Actual Cost Each	Actual Cost Total
HOME/FOOD STORAGE INVENTORY Worksheet #43 Date:										

CHERRY PICKING	Worksheet #44	Store A	Store B	Store C
Item	Size	@ Cost	@ Cost	@ Cost

"BEST PRICE" BOX Worksheet #45

1. Collect: One 3" x 5" card box
    2 sets of A-Z 3" x 5" card dividers (two different colors, one
           for FOOD/FOOD STORAGE and one for HOME
           STORAGE)
    200 lined 3" x 5" cards

2. Line 200 3" x 5" cards into six columns, one wide and five narrow.
    Headings for each column can be added as shown in the example below.

Item	Brand	Size	Price	Store	Date
Aluminum Foil	Rey.	25'	$.50	Safe.	7/00

3. The first set of A-Z dividers is for FOOD and FOOD STORAGE items.
    These are kept in front of the second set of dividers as they are used
    more often. The second set of A-Z dividers is for NON-FOOD items (i.e.
    HOME STORAGE items).

4. Use one 3" x 5" card per item. Fill out the card when a good price is
    noted in the ads or after a good purchase. Record information in each
    category. For example: Aluminum, Reynolds, 25 sq. ft., $.50, Safeway,
    07/2007

5. File the card in the proper section, behind the right 3" x 5" card divider.

6. Use the "Best Price" Box each time ads are being reviewed. Watch for
    items which meet or beat the previous best price.

7. Use the "Best Price" Box each time a shopping trip is made. Compare
    store prices with the information in the "Best Price" Box. Try to beat or
    meet the previous "best price" in all purchases made.

Chapter Twenty-Four

OFFICE SUPPLIES LIST

"To do the right job, you must have the right tools and plenty of them".
Marie C. Ricks

SUPPLIES NEEDED: Attached **Worksheets #75, #76, #77, #78, #79, #80, #81,** and **#82** give a complete office supplies list of items needed to accomplish the organizational tasks in this book

GOALS: Review supply lists

Choose either to approach the projects by "topic" or "item"

Collect or purchase the needed supplies

Set aside small portions of time each day during the next several weeks to assemble and prepare the different "tools" which will make your life better and your family more organized

Occasionally in class, a student will get frustrated.
"All you do is use 3" x 5" cards, binders, and forms," she said. "I want to know just what you expect me to buy to get through all these projects with just one stop at the office supply store."
"No," said another. "That won't work for me. I work on just one project at a time and I need to know exactly what to get for that one project. My husband's salary only lets me go so fast. I don't want all the 'good' news at once."
And so with those needs in mind, the "Office Supplies List" was developed.

Getting it together all at once can be very difficult. At the same time, when you are at the store and want to purchase the supplies you need, sometimes it is nice to know just exactly how many of this and that you will need to do one project (or even all of them) right.

Attached are two lists. One is an office supply list by "TOPIC" and the other is a list by "ITEM". Choose whichever best suits your lifestyle and pocket book and go to work. Time spent now will save much time and energy later.

OFFICE SUPPLIES LIST – *BY TOPIC* Worksheet #75

Topic	Amount Needed	Item
Calendaring	1	Calendar, large wall
	10	Set of colored marking pens
Files	1	3" x 5" card box (small)
	5+	3" x 5" blank card dividers
	50	3" x 5" lined cards
	10	Letter-size manila folders
Finances	1	2"-wide 8-1/2" x 11" 3-ring binder
	10	8-1/2" x 11" binder dividers
	100	8-1/2" x 11" columnar sheets
	25	8-1/2" x 11" cardstock
	1	Zippered pencil case
Food Management/ Food Storage: "Best Price" Box	1	3" x 5" card box (small), also used for Home Storage "Best Price" 3" x 5" cards
	27	3" x 5" card dividers, alphabetized (a different color than the Home Storage "Best Price" card dividers)
	100	3" x 5" lined cards

Topic	Amount Needed	Item
Food Management: "Recipe" Box and Binder	1	3" x 5" card box (small)
	7	3" x 5" card dividers, blank
	2	Sets of "recipe" card dividers
	50	3" x 5" lined cards
	1	1"-wide 8-1/2" x 11" 3-ring binder
	25	8-1/2" x 11" sheet protectors
	15+	8-1/2" x 11" binder dividers
"Greeting Cards" Binder	1	2"-wide 8-1/2" x 11" 3-ring binder
	20	8-1/2" x 11" binder folders with pockets
Home Storage: "Best Price" Box	1	3" x 5" card box (small), also used for Food Management/ Food Storage "Best Price" 3" x 5" cards
	27	3" x 5" card dividers, alphabetized (another color than the Food Storage "Best Price" cards)
	100	3" x 5" lined cards
Housecleaning Plan: the "Brain" Box	1	3" x 5" card box (large), also used for "Lists" 3" x 5" cards
	21	3" x 5" blank card dividers
	150	3" x 5" lined cards

Topic	Amount Needed	Item
Family "Information" Binder	1	2"-wide 8-1/2" x 11" 3-ring binder
	20 or more	8-1/2" x 11" binder dividers
	1	Clear plastic binder-size business card holder (kept behind the "Keys" divider)
Lists	1	3" x 5" card box (large) also used for "Brain" Box 3" x 5" cards
	9	3" x 5" blank card dividers
	100	3" x 5" lined cards
"Sources" Binder	1	1"-wide 8-1/2" x 11" 3-ring binder
	27	8-1/2" x 11" dividers, alphabetized
Time Management: Planner	1	1"-wide 8-1/2" x 5-1/2" binder
	9	8-1/2" x 5-1/2" binder dividers
	25	8-1/2 x 5-1/2" lined notepaper
Training Children	25	3" x 5" lined cards

Topic	Amount Needed	Item
Trivia	1	2' x 3' corkboard
	1	Rotating address file
	5	3" x 5" lined cards (for phone numbers placed near the phone)

Item	Amount Needed	Referenced Topic(s)
8-1/2" x 11" 3-ring binders	1	Finances: "Finances" Binder (2" wide)
	1	Food Management: "Recipes" Binder (1" wide)
	1	Family "Information" Binder (2" wide)
	1	"Greetings Cards" Binder (2" wide)
	1	"Sources" Binder (1" wide)
8-1/2" x 11" binder dividers	10	Finances: "Finances" Binder (blank dividers)
	15	Food Management: "Recipes" Binder (blank dividers)
	20+	Family "Information" Binder (blank dividers)
	27	"Sources" Binder (alphabetized dividers)
8-1/2" x 11" binder dividers with pockets	20	"Greetings Cards" Binder
8-1/2" x 11" clear sheet protectors	25	Food Management: "Recipes" Binder

Item	Amount Needed	Referenced Topic(s)
8-1/2" x 11" clear plastic	1	Family "Information" Binder (behind business card holder the "Keys" divider)
3" x 5" card box (large) (preferably shoe-box shaped)	1	Housecleaning Plan: The "Brain" Box, Lists
3" x 5" card box (small)	1	Files: "Find a File" Box
3" x 5" card box (small) Storage, and Home Storage:	1	Food Management, Food "Best Price" Box
3" x 5" card box (small or large)	1	Food Management: "Recipe" Box
3" x 5" card dividers	5+	Files (blank dividers)
	7	Food Management: "Recipe" Box (blank dividers)
	2 sets	Food Management: "Recipe" Box ("recipe" style dividers)
	27	Food Management/ Food Storage: "Best Price" Box (alphabetized dividers)
	27	Home Storage: "Best Price" Box (alphabetized dividers)
	21	Housecleaning Plan: the "Brain" Box (blank dividers)
	9+	Lists (blank dividers)

Item	Amount Needed	Referenced Topic(s)
3" x 5" lined cards	50	Files: "Find a File" Box
	100	Food Management, Food Storage, and Home Storage: "Best Price" Box
	50	Food Management: "Recipe" Box
	150	Housecleaning Plan: The "Brain" Box
	100	Lists
	25	Training Children
	5	Trivia
8-1/2" x 5-1/2" 3-ring binder	1	Time Management: Planner
8-1/2" x 5-1/2" binder dividers	9	Time Management: Planner
8-1/2 x 5-1/2" lined notepaper	25	Time Management: Planner
Calendar, large wall	1	Calendaring
Set of colored marking pens	10	Calendaring
8-1/2" x 11" 3-columned columnar sheets	100	Finances: "Finances" Binder
8-1/2" x 11" cardstock	25	Finances: "Finances" Binder

Item	Amount Needed	Referenced Topic(s)
Zippered pencil case	1	Finances: "Finances" Binder
Letter-size manila folders	10+	Files
Rotating address file	1	Trivia
2' x 3' Corkboard	1	Trivia

House of Order

1. Decide which of the following items you wish to order:

Description	Quantity	Unit Price	Shipping/ handling	Total
1) House of Order Handbook - *200+ pages of solid information and numerous forms to get you organized now and forever*		$20.00	$23.00	$
2) Organization for the Almost Organized *Book - 100+ pages of additional wisdom for home managers in all seasons of their lives*		$12.00	$15.00	$
3) Master Menu Cookbook - *50+ pages of great, simple recipes to get your Master Menu working every day of the week*		$ 6.00	$ 8.00	$
4) Housecleaning Plan *3" x 5" cards - 40 sheet packet (makes 160 cards) which detail how to keep your house neat and clean all the time*		$ 6.00	$ 8.00	$
5) Training Children to Work *3" x 5" cards - 45 sheet packet (makes 180 cards) which detail essential skills for children and teenagers to learn*		$ 6.00	$ 8.00	$
6) 200 clear, plastic 3" x 5" card **slipcovers** (to keep everything clean) *when you purchase the* **Housecleaning Plan** *packet or* **Training Children to Work** *packet*		$ 6.00	$8.00	$
7) Best Prices *3" x 5" cards - 40 sheet packet (makes 160 cards) to help you track the best prices every time you shop*		$ 6.00	$ 8.00	$
8) Family Information Binder - *forms for a family of eight - 75 sheets to track important information you need to run a family*		$ 6.00	$ 8.00	$
9) Cleaning Cards - *five 8.5 x 11" heavy-duty laminated sheets which detail the essentials needed to get household jobs done right (whether you want the rooms "fast" cleaned or "deep" cleaned)*		$ 6.00	$ 8.00	$
10) Cartooning Fun *Book - 50+ pages of creative fun which teaches simple cartooning techniques to develop creativity in children and bring their self-expression to higher level (for children 5 to 500)*		$ 6.00	$8.00	$
TOTAL				$

2. Please fill out the information below:

Name: _____

Address: _____

_____

3. Send this order form and your CHECK to:

Marie C. Ricks, 6756 West 10050 North, Highland, Utah 84003
or see **www.houseoforder.com** for other payment options!

214   HOUSE OF ORDER - OFFICE SUPPLIES LIST

House of Order

1. **Decide which of the following items you wish to order:**

Description	Quantity	Unit Price	Shipping/ handling	Total
1) House of Order Handbook - *200+ pages of solid information and numerous forms to get you organized now and forever*		$20.00	$23.00	$
2) Organization for the Almost Organized *Book - 100+ pages of additional wisdom for home managers in all seasons of their lives*		$12.00	$15.00	$
3) Master Menu Cookbook - *50+ pages of great, simple recipes to get your Master Menu working every day of the week*		$ 6.00	$ 8.00	$
4) Housecleaning Plan *3" x 5" cards - 40 sheet packet (makes 160 cards) which detail how to keep your house neat and clean all the time*		$ 6.00	$ 8.00	$
5) Training Children to Work *3" x 5" cards - 45 sheet packet (makes 180 cards) which detail essential skills for children and teenagers to learn*		$ 6.00	$ 8.00	$
6) *200 clear, plastic 3" x 5" card* **slipcovers** *(to keep everything clean) when you purchase the* **Housecleaning Plan** *packet or* **Training Children to Work** *packet*		$ 6.00	$8.00	$
7) Best Prices *3" x 5" cards - 40 sheet packet (makes 160 cards) to help you track the best prices every time you shop*		$ 6.00	$ 8.00	$
8) Family Information Binder - *forms for a family of eight - 75 sheets to track important information you need to run a family*		$ 6.00	$ 8.00	$
9) Cleaning Cards - *five 8.5 x 11" heavy-duty laminated sheets which detail the essentials needed to get household jobs done right (whether you want the rooms "fast" cleaned or "deep" cleaned)*		$ 6.00	$ 8.00	$
10) Cartooning Fun *Book - 50+ pages of creative fun which teaches simple cartooning techniques to develop creativity in children and bring their self-expression to higher level (for children 5 to 500)*		$ 6.00	$8.00	$
TOTAL				$

2. **Please fill out the information below:**

    Name: _____

    Address: _____

    _____

3. **Send this order form and your CHECK to:**

    Marie C. Ricks, 6756 West 10050 North, Highland, Utah 84003
    or see **www.houseoforder.com** for other payment options!